TUGS IN COLOUR - WORLDWIDE

by

Andrew Wiltshire

The West German ocean-going tug **Pacific** was owned by Bugsier-, Reederei- und Bergungs- GmbH, of Hamburg. The origins of Bugsier date back to 1866 as a ship owner based at Hamburg, but they eventually become involved in the salvage business. Bugsier entered into harbour towage at Hamburg in 1952. The **Pacific** was a rather splendid looking tug completed in 1962 by F Schichau GmbH at Bremerhaven. She had an overall length of 236 feet and a beam of 39 feet and her gross tonnage was recorded as 1093. Her main engines were a pair of 12-cylinder Klockner-Humboldt-Deiutz of 6000bhp, driving propellers in Kort nozzles. This gave her a bollard pull of 72 tonnes and a speed of 15.5 knots. She is seen here at anchor off St Anthony head near Falmouth on 8 July 1973. During her career the **Pacific** attended many salvage operations around the world including the stricken tanker **Amoco Cadiz** off the coast of Brittany in March 1978. The **Pacific** was sold in 1984 to become **Inter-Gulf** for Gencom Shipping Ltd, of Gibraltar. From 1986 she became the Panamanian-flag **Imsalv Lion**, whilst her final name was **Seabulk Princess** for owners in Dubai. She was broken up at Gadani Beach in early 2001. Bugsier's tugs were always immaculate and always a credit to their owner.

(John Wiltshire)

INTRODUCTION

The tug has played an important role around the world for well over a century and continues to do so to this day. This humble workhorse has evolved from a simple, reliable and often fairly small vessel in its early days, to a sophisticated, specialised and usually very powerful piece of engineering in the 21st century. All around the world they continue to fulfil the roles of harbour tugs, ocean-going and salvage tugs right through to the more specialised inland waterway vessels. This book will hopefully become a pictorial reminder of some of the types of tugs that have worked in the last fifty years or so.

Tugs are instantly recognisable, but upon closer inspection it soon becomes apparent that they come in all shapes and sizes, and this is often reflected in their country of origin. In this book I have tried to include a good selection of tugs from all corners of the world, some old and some modern, and working in many different environments. Unfortunately, some areas, especially African nations, have proved impossible to represent due to a complete lack of suitable material.

Some abbreviations used throughout are: grt (gross registered tonnage), bhp (brake horse power) and ihp (indicated horsepower).

Acknowledgements

This book has been at the back of my mind for a number of years, and the opportunity to compile this title has given me a lot of pleasure over the last twelve months or so. Many thanks must go to Nigel Jones and Douglas Cromby for their efforts in getting the project started. A big thank you must also go out to all the other contributors including Simon Smith, Jim McFaul, Réne Beauchamp, K Brzoza (Risto) and Guillermo C Berger for the time and effort they have willingly given to my requests for help.

As with my earlier books, one of the great inputs has come from my friend Kevin Blair on Tyneside who has spent much time chasing up various queries I have raised on individual tugs. Finally, as always, I am grateful to Bernard McCall for his support and Gil Mayes for checking the captions, and of course my wife Tracey, for letting me spend numerous evenings alone at the computer, putting words to captions, and thumbing through books and records.

Written sources used throughout include copies of Ian Allan *Coastal Ships*, *Lekko* and *Ships Monthly* magazines, *Lloyd's Register* publications, *Tugs: 3000hp and over* (Lekko) and various books about tugs including *150 Years of the Maltese Cross* (Proud) and the WSS publications *Empire Tugs*, *Hamburg Tugs* and *Cory Towage Ltd*.

Andrew Wiltshire   *Cardiff*   *March 2014*

Published by Bernard McCall, 400 Nore Road, Portishead, Bristol, BS20 8EZ, England. Website: www.coastalshipping.co.uk
Telephone/fax: 01275 846178   E-mail: bernard@coastalshipping.co.uk All distribution enquiries should be addressed to the publisher.

Printed by Amadeus Press, Ezra House, West 26 Business Park, Cleckheaton, West Yorkshire, BD19 4TQ, England. Website: www.amadeuspress.co.uk
Telephone: 01274 863210   Fax: 01274 863211   E-mail: info@amadeuspress.co.uk

ISBN: 978-1-902953-63-2.

Front cover: The steam tug **Sir William Hoy** was named after a Scottish-born gentleman who had left the UK for South Africa in 1890, and went on to become the General Manager of the South African Railways. **Sir William Hoy** was a fine-looking tug that entered service at Durban in 1929 with the South African Government (Railways and Harbours Administration). She was the last tug to be built on the River Tyne by Armstrong Whitworth Co Ltd, and was the only one to be completed at the Willington Quay yard, Newcastle. The **Sir William Hoy** was an impressive 180 feet long with a gross tonnage of 786, and was of twin-screw layout. Her boilers were coal-fired and supplied steam to a pair of Armstrong Whitworth triple expansion steam engines of 3500ihp. She had a service speed of 11 knots. At some stage later in her working life, a single fire-fighting monitor was added, mounted on a small platform forward of her accommodation. This superb action shot of her was taken at Durban in May 1974, and she was dressed overall to celebrate the 150th anniversary of the founding of the City of Durban. During the 1970s and 1980s, these fine steam tugs were gradually replaced by modern and compact diesel-powered tractor tugs at all South African ports and in due course the **Sir William Hoy** was laid up at Durban from 1980. An attempt was made to save her, but she eventually succumbed to the breakers at Durban in 1982.

(Trevor Jones)

Back cover: Towage at the port of Ravenna on Italy's Adriatic coast is provided by Societa Esercizio Rimorchi E Salvataggi SERS Srl which became part of the GESMAR Group in the 1980s. GESMAR serve ten Italian ports and operate in the region of thirty-six tugs ranging from conventional single-screw tugs to modern stern-drive and tractor tugs. The **Riccardo** and her sistership **Alessandro Secondo** were completed in 1991 by the Italian shipyard Cooperativa Metallurgica Ing G Tommasi Cantiere Navale Sl of Ancona. They were single-screw tugs fitted with Ulstein controllable-pitch propellers giving a service speed of 12 knots and a bollard pull of 34 tonnes. Power was obtained from an 8-cylinder Wärtsilä (Nohab) diesel developing 2067bhp. Both tugs had a gross tonnage of 181 and accommodation for a crew of seven. This view of the **Riccardo** was taken at Marina di Ravenna on 20 September 1998. An interesting tug still on fleet strength in 2012 was the **Gatto** of 1958 which was originally the British-owned **Banbury Cross** of Tees Towing, an early example of a Voith Schneider tractor.

(Nigel Jones)

About a dozen motor tugs were delivered to the Belgian fleet of Union de Remorquage et de Sauvetage S.A. (URS) between 1958 and 1963, with most being distributed between Remorquage Letzer and SA de Remorquage à Hélice subsidiaries based at Antwerp. The **Marguerite Gerling**, often referred to as **Marg. Gerling**, was delivered to the latter fleet in March 1961 from her builder J Boel and Zoon at Temse on the River Scheldt. She had a gross tonnage of 136 and was powered by a 1000bhp Deutz diesel. In 1974 she became an integral part of the URS and was heavily rebuilt in 1979 following a collision. In 1991 the

Marguerite Gerling was sold to Willem Muller BV, of Terneuzen, becoming **Zeeland**. Willem Muller operated an interesting fleet of motor tugs having served Terneuzen and the Ghent Canal since 1911. In this view we see her underway off Terneuzen on 17 August 1993. By 1999 she had passed to the Grimsby-based fleet of Survey and Supply as the **Ella** before being moved to Hartlepool in 2002 for use as a floating restaurant. After trading for a while as such, it is believed to have closed and in 2013 is thought to be for sale.

(Marc Piché)

The Cheshire shipyard of W J Yarwood & Sons Ltd, Northwich, completed its final vessel in November 1965, after which the business closed down. The **St. Elmo** was the last in a long line of tugs built by Yarwood and was delivered to Maltese owner Midmed Towage Co Ltd of Valletta, the only tug they ever bought new. She was 100 feet in length with a gross tonnage of 168 and her main engine was a 6-cylinder Ruston and Hornsby of 1440bhp. In October 1980 the fleets of Midmed Towage Co Ltd and Malta Ship Towage Co Ltd (MST) were nationalised by the Maltese government and merged to form Tug Malta Ltd. The **St. Elmo** was renamed **Katrin**. Here we see her underway in the Grand Harbour at Valletta on 28 September 1992. Since the year 2000 Tug Malta has been gradually modernising its fleet and the **Katrin** was replaced in 2002. She was sold that year to another Maltese owner Piscopo A & A of Marsaxlokk who adapted her for use in the fishing industry, and as such took the new name **Murkurt**. By 2011 she was working for Emma Navigation Ltd, Tarxien, and was reported to still be in service during 2013.

(Nigel Jones)

Celtic Tugs Ltd was founded in 1995 to provide towage in the River Shannon and Shannon estuary, and also along the west coast of Ireland. In 2000 a contract was secured for the provision of three ASD-type tugs to service this area, these being the **Celtic Rebel**, **Celtic Isle** and **Celtic Banner**, all of which are Japanese-built vessels. As such the tugs are operated by Celtic Tugs Ltd, Cork, for the Irish Mainport Group. The **Celtic Rebel** was built in 1984 by Daikoo Dockyard Co Ltd, Osaka, for Takemaru Kaiun KK of Osaka as the **Take Maru No. 71**. She has a gross tonnage of 309 and an overall length of 123 feet and is equipped for fire-fighting and salvage. Her main propulsion consists of two fixed-pitch Z-Peller type ZP-3A units, driven by a pair of 6-cylinder Niigata diesels developing a total of 3500bhp. This gives her a bollard pull of 48 tonnes and a speed of 13.5 knots. The **Celtic Rebel** can also boast accommodation for two officers, six crew and twelve passengers. She is seen at Foynes, County Limerick, on 27 May 2003, a location where Celtic Tugs provide towage for ships visiting the port.

(Dominic McCall)

This rather pleasant setting is on the Stockholm archipelago on 18 June 1978 and was taken from the Russian cruise ship *Litva*. The *Bull* is an icebreaking tug of 276 tons gross, and was built in 1972 by A/B Asi-Verken at Åmål on Lake Vänern. Her hull is constructed to Ice class 1 classification which would be essential for use in the Baltic during the winter months. The *Bull* is powered by a 9-cylinder 2-stroke Nohab Polar diesel of 2476bhp which drives a controllable-pitch propeller. She was delivered new to Kran and Bogserings A/B at Stockholm.

In 1977 this fleet passed to Göteborgs Bogserings and Bärgnings A/B of Goteborg together with the *Bull*. She continued to work in Stockholm but now alongside tugs like the *Karl* and *Per*. Further changes of ownership saw the *Bull* passing in 1985 from A/B Neptun Röda Bolaget, of Stockholm, to Sundsvalls Hamnförvaltning A/B, of Sundsvall. She retained her existing name but her port of registry changed to Sundsvall. She remains active with this owner in 2012 as their only tug.

(John Wiltshire)

The **Minotavros** is a fine example of a former British motor tug that continues to earn her keep in Greek waters, and is kept in immaculate condition. She is operated by Minos Shipping Co and is managed by Jas John Adamis & Spyros Athousakis, being based at the port of Heraklion on the Greek island of Crete. She began life in 1960 as the **Plumgarth** and, along with her sister **Avongarth**, was completed by W J Yarwood & Sons Ltd, of Northwich, in Cheshire for R & J H Rea Ltd of Bristol, for service at Avonmouth. As built she had a gross tonnage of 156 and was powered by a 8-cylinder Ruston & Hornsby diesel of 870bhp. As **Plumgarth** she was soon transferred to South Wales where she worked at both Cardiff and Barry, passing to Cory Ship Towage Ltd in 1970. The **Avongarth** remained at Avonmouth until 1979, when both tugs were transferred to the Plymouth fleet. In 1985 the **Plumgarth** was sold to her present owner and has subsequently been slightly modified. She has lost her flying bridge and her main mast has been relocated to her funnel. Her traditional lifeboat has been replaced by a dinghy and a fire-fighting monitor can be found mounted on a new post aft of her funnel. We see her here at Heraklion on 25 December 1996.

(Nigel Jones)

6

In 1978 United Towing Ltd of Hull took delivery of two identical ocean-going salvage tugs, the *Irishman* followed by the *Yorkshireman*, both coming from the yard of Cochrane Shipbuilders Ltd of Selby. They were twin-screw vessels and had controllable-pitch propellers in Kort nozzles and a controllable-pitch bow thruster unit. Hull dimensions were 138 feet overall length with a beam of 38 feet and the original gross tonnage was recorded as 641. The main engines were a pair of 12-cylinder vee-type Ruston diesels of 4380bhp which gave the tugs a bollard pull of approximately 70 tonnes. The *Irishman* was delivered new to United Towing (Euroman) Ltd and put to work worldwide. In April 1982 she was requisitioned to support the Falklands Task Force service, and continued to play a role in the South Atlantic until her contract expired in 1986. In this view she is seen at Port Stanley in the Falkland Islands in 1986. By now her gross tonnage had risen to 686, and her registered owner was United Towing (Drake) Ltd. In 1988 the *Irishman* was sold to Semco Salvage Co Ltd, Singapore and renamed *Salvision*, and again in 1993 to Pacific Carriers of Singapore, who renamed her *Pacnav Ace*. Later the same year she moved over to the Mexican flag, joining the fleet of Naviera Armamex SA de CV, Ciudad del Carmen, and gaining the new name *El Huasteco*. Twenty years later in 2013, she was still sailing as *El Huasteco*.

(Jeff Screeton)

Bukser & Bjergningsselskapet A/S of Oslo have been operating tugs in Norway and Scandinavian waters since 1913. One hundred years later they continue to serve Oslo and other Norwegian ports with a modern fleet of about twenty tugs. One of the smaller tugs to have sailed for Bukser & Bjergningsselskapet was the *Frier* which is seen at Oslo on 4 July 2000. At this time she was forty-one years old, but has benefitted from much updating over the years. The *Frier* was built in 1959 in the Netherlands by FA G de Vries Lentsch Schpswerf. "Het Fort", Amsterdam for service with Norwegian owner Frierfjordens Iskasse of Porsgrunn near Larvik, and managed by Porsgrunn Harbour Office. At 72 feet in length she had a gross tonnage of 110 and was classed as an icebreaking tug. As built she was fitted with an 8-cylinder A/S Bergens M/V (Normo) diesel of 545bhp and had a speed of 10 knots. In 1967 the *Frier* was re-engined with an 8-cylinder Deutz with a much more useful output of 1200bhp. Twelve years later her managers became Bukser & Bjergningsselskapet A/S and she was eventually based in Oslo. In 2005 the *Frier* was sold to Noås Nordmuddring A/B, of Örnsköldsvik, as *Leam* becoming *Heros* in 2008 for Swedish owner Tugab A/B, Gävle. In 2011 she became *Tug Frier*, this time for Kragerø Marine Services, and sailing under the Norwegian flag.

(John Wiltshire)

The Finnish tug **Meteor** makes a fine sight as she negotiates the ice at Turku on 25 February 2010. She is actually quite an old ship at fifty years of age but has been subject to some rebuilding which at some stage has included a new wheelhouse and most probably the addition of the bow-thruster unit. She was built as the ice-breaking salvage tug **Meteor** in 1960 by OY Laivateollisuus AB of Turku for Finska Bergnings A/B Neptun, Helsinki. She had a gross tonnage of 352 and an overall length of 117 feet. Her main engine was an 8-cylinder diesel of 1201bhp, built by Crossley Bros Ltd, which gave her a speed of 13.5 knots. She was renamed **Pellinki** in 1977 and in 1981 was sold to the Government of the Republic of Finland for use by the Finnish Navy, and given the name **Parainen**. By the 1990s, her gross tonnage increased to 396 and as such she continued to work as a salvage and rescue tug. She also received a replacement engine in the form of a Wärtsilä 8R22MD-D. In 2001 the **Parainen** was sold by the Finnish Navy to Finnish owner ET Merenkulkukoulutus and regained her original name **Meteor** once more. By 2006 she was owned by Rauma Chartering and Towage Agency OY AB Ltd, who operate ten tugs on harbour and coastal towing work around Finland and in the Baltic.

(K Brzoza)

The next two images are of Polish tugs that are only five years apart in age, but are actually very different types of vessel. The **Mis** dates from 1970 and was built in Poland by Gdynska Stocznia Remontowa at Gdynia for the Polish Government, and managed by the Zarzad Portu Gdansk at Gdansk. Her hull which has an overall length of 83 feet and a breadth of 22 feet, was constructed to work in ice and she has gross tonnage of 115. The **Mis** is a single-screw tug with a bow-thruster unit, and is powered by a 6-cylinder diesel manufactured by VEB Schwermasch. "Karl Liebknecht" developing 800bhp. From 1985 her owner became the Morski Port Handlowy Gdansk SA, and she continued to operate from Gdansk. In 1993 she passed to WUZ Port & Maritime Services Co Ltd, Gdansk, and by early 2003 had been reported as being laid up at Gdynia. However, this shot of the **Mis** taken on 6 August 2003 at Gdansk shows her to be still active. By 2010 she had become the **Jarek** and was still working at Gdansk.

(Bernard McCall)

The **Slon** was one of a pair of Voith Schneider-type tractor tugs delivered to Zarzad Portu Gdansk at Gdansk in 1975. Her sister was the **Bobr** and both were of fairly typical layout for this type of tug with a large foredeck, and the towing hook located well aft. Both tugs were 111grt and had hull dimensions of 79 feet overall length with a maximum beam of just under 23 feet. They were twin-unit Voith Schneider tractors, with a bollard pull of 10.5 tonnes and both tugs were powered by a pair of 6-cylinder Russkiy type 6CH24/34 diesels developing 900bhp. Like the **Mis**, the **Slon** passed to Morski Port Handlowy Gdansk in 1985 and later to "WUZ Co Ltd", Gdansk. The **Slon** is also seen at Gdansk on 6 August 2003. In 2012 both the **Slon** and the **Bobr** were still hard at work with WUZ, who operate about a dozen tugs at Gdansk.

(Bernard McCall)

Yugoslavia became a communist state in 1946 and remained so until the Yugoslav Wars commenced in 1991. At this time the Republic of Croatia as we know it today declared its independence from Yugoslavia, and ultimately resulted in a successful outcome. Today the major port in Croatia is Rijeka. The **Lukas** was an addition to the fleet of Jadranski Pomorski Servis DD in May 2009 and is based in Rijeka. They are the main tug provider at Rijeka, while back in the days of Yugoslavia, the principal operator was Poduzece "Luka". The **Lukas** is seen at her home port when quite new in November 2009. She is a Damen STANTUG of design 2608, and was built in Cuba under licence by Damex Shipbuilding &

Engineering AVV of Santiago de Cuba. The **Lukas** incorporates a pair of Promarin fixed-pitch propellers that rotate in Van de Giessen Optima nozzles which give her a bollard pull ahead of approximately 50 tonnes and a service speed of 12 knots. Her main engines are two 12-cyl Caterpillar type 3512BTA diesels with a combined output of 3500bhp. In addition, she is equipped for fire-fighting and has air-conditioned accommodation for up to eight crew members. Jadranski Pomorski Servis also own nine other tugs including **David Prvi** of 2002 and **Mak** of 2006.

(Dominic McCall)

The last twin-screw steam tugs delivered to the Republic of South Africa (Railways and Harbours Administration) were three vessels completed at the Scottish shipyard Ferguson Bros (Port Glasgow) Ltd of Port Glasgow near Greenock on the Clyde. The first of these was the *Danie Hugo* which was completed in March 1959 and was followed by the *F. C. Sturrock* later that year, the final tug being the *J. R. More* which was delivered in 1961. The *Danie Hugo* was named after a railway commissioner and was based at Cape Town for a large part of her working life along with the *F. C. Sturrock*. This is where we see her in December 1974 with the famous landmark Table Mountain in the background. The *Danie Hugo* had a gross tonnage of 812 and was an impressive 176 feet in length. She was oil-fired and her machinery consisted of a pair of triple expansion steam reciprocating engines of 3100ihp built by Rankin and Blackmore Ltd of Greenock. The *Danie Hugo* was eventually broken up at Walvis Bay in 1984, but the story doesn't end there. A large part of her accommodation was moved to Swakopmund where it was incorporated into a restaurant at the Jetty Area. Named the *Tug Restaurant*, diners would be able to enjoy à la carte food at this idyllic location, while seated in part of an old steam tug.

(Trevor Jones)

Turkey has become a leading tug-building nation in the last twenty years or so, completing vessels for overseas customers as well as for its home market. The **Kurtarma 1**, together with its sister the **Kurtarma 2**, were constructed in 2000 in Izmir by Turkiye Gemi Sanayii AS (Alaybey shipyard). They are powerful twin-unit Voith Schneider tractor tugs of 451grt and with an overall length of 112 feet and a beam of 37 feet. The **Kurtarma 1** was delivered in May 2000 to her owner, who is described by the title Kiyi Eminyeti ve Gemicilik Kurtarma Isletmesi Genel Mudurlugu Gemicilik kur Dairesi BSK of Istanbul, but also described elsewhere as Turkish Government (Coastal Safety & Salvage Administration). Both tugs are fitted for fire-fighting and are each powered by a pair of 6-cylinder Caterpillar diesels of 5098bhp which give them a speed of 14 knots. Four more tugs followed, again with Voith Schneider propulsion, but this time larger. These were the **Kurtarma 3** and **Kurtarma 4** in 2004 and the **Kurtarma 5** and **Kurtarma 6** in 2008. The **Kurtarma 1** is seen at Istanbul on 4 July 2010, and makes a nice contrast with the steam tug **Liman 2** on page 23.

(Douglas Cromby)

The Gulf of Aqaba lies at the northern end of the Red Sea and located on the upper shores of the Gulf can be found the Jordanian city and ancient port of Aqaba. In 2006 a new and much larger port was opened to the south of the old city. Aqaba Port Authority operated at least three ship-handling tugs for many years, which included the **Karameh** and **Safi** of 1983. In 2008 the first of four new tugs to serve the new larger port was delivered to Aqaba Port Marine Services Company (APMS). The **Irbid** and **Mafraq** were built in China by Bonny Fair Development at the shipyard of Guangzhou Panyu Lingnan Shipbuilding Co Ltd, of Guangzhou. They were 216grt stern-drive tugs of 2028bhp, each being powered by a pair of 8-cylinder Caterpillar diesels. The following year a slightly larger pair at 288grt, the **Amman** and **Aqaba** were completed by the same yard. These were more powerful tugs at 3548bhp and were powered by 12-cylinder Caterpillar diesels giving them a bollard pull of 45 tonnes. All four were fitted for fire-fighting, and in this view of 4 March 2011 we see one of each type, the **Mafraq** and the **Aqaba**.

(Andrew Wiltshire collection)

The end of the civil war in Lebanon in 1990 saw the port at Beirut gradually return to normality and develop into a busy commercial facility. By 1993 a tug operation was established by Hassan Baltagi and Ali Tabbit at the port, and traded as Beirut Pilots. The first tug purchased was the **Baltagi V** which was previously Alexandra Towing's **Huskisson** of 1968. This was followed in 1995 by the **Baltagi VI** which came from Lawson Batey Tugs of Newcastle, and was the former **Northsider** of 1967. The **Baltagi XX** was acquired in 2000 and also came from the Tyne where she had worked as the **Cragsider**, latterly with Cory Towage Ltd. As the **Cragsider** she had been launched on 8 September 1976 for Lawson Batey Tugs

Ltd, Newcastle from the shipyard of Richard Dunston Ltd at Hessle on the Humber. She was a tug of gross tonnage 266 with an overall length of 107 feet, and powered by a 6-cylinder Mirrlees KMR6-type diesel developing 3140bhp. This was geared to a fixed-pitch propeller within a steerable Kort nozzle, giving the tug a bollard pull of 45 tonnes. The Lawson Batey business passed to Clyde Shipping Co Ltd in April 1983, which passed in turn to Cory Towage Ltd in May 1995. The Cory fleet was taken over by Wijsmuller in 2000 and the **Cragsider** left the fleet at this point. In this view she is seen at Beirut on 18 June 2001. The **Baltagi XX** is believed to be still active in 2013.

(Nigel Jones)

The shipyard of Yarrows Ltd at Esquimalt, Victoria, was responsible for completing the **Kingcome**, the first large steel-hulled tug newly constructed in British Columbia following World War Two. She was delivered in 1952 to the Kingcome Navigation Co Ltd, which was a subsidiary of the Powell River Company and was registered in Vancouver. The **Kingcome** was a fine-looking tug with a gross tonnage of 242, an overall length of 100 feet and was powered by a 950bhp engine from the Union Diesel Eng Co. She had a high standard of accommodation and was said to be a very stable vessel. She was mainly used for towing log rafts and rail barges, and could be found operating in locations such as Alert Bay and Powell River. In 1969 her main engine was replaced by a 16-cylinder Caterpillar D399 diesel. The **Kingcome** appears to be in excellent condition in this view of her dating from April 1995. She continued towing until about 2000 when she suffered a broken crankshaft. By then she was owned by the Washington Marine Group which sold her for conversion into a private yacht. This duly took place and she emerged as such under the name **Charlotte Queen**.

(Don Brown)

Rimorchaitori Riuniti Panfido & Co SpA have been operating harbour tugs at Venice since well before the World War Two, the origins of the company going back to 1880. During the 1950s many Italian tug operators were still putting their faith in steam-powered tugs for their new tonnage, but Panfido & Co opted for new motor tugs from 1957. The **Novus** was one of the first Voith Schneider tractor tugs to be built for an Italian tug fleet, and was delivered to Rimorchaitori Riuniti Panfido & Co SpA in 1964. She was built at the yard of NV Scheepswerven v/h HH Bodewes, Millingen a/d Rijn in the Netherlands, and closely resembled some of the tugs completed at this time for the NV Nieuwe Rotterdamse Sleepdienst fleet. The **Novus** was 92 feet in length with a beam of 27 feet and was completed with a gross tonnage of 151. She had a pair of Voith Schneider cycloidal propulsion units that were driven by two 8-cylinder Deutz diesels of 1200bhp. This particular tug must have made a good impression in her home port of Venice as a further two examples, the **Geminus** and **Pardus**, were delivered in 1966, followed by the **Squalus** in 1967 and the **Emilio Panfido** in 1969. This shot of the **Novus** was taken at Venice in May 1970, at a time when the fleet was still operating three splendid steam tugs. During the 1990s, the fleet assumed the title CMV Rimorchiatori Riuniti Panfido & Co, and a new livery was adopted for the tugs.

(the late T W Wiltshire)

Traditionally, many major Indian ports have been served by tugs operated by the local port authority, a situation which continues to this day. There are also a number of private companies providing tugs for ship-handling and dredging operations. Great Offshore Ltd (GOL), based in Mumbai, have a presence in almost all major Indian ports including Mumbai, Tuticorin and New Mangalore, and operate a fleet of around twelve harbour tugs as well as a number of anchor-handling tugs and supply vessels. Between the years 1997 and 2000 a class of six modern stern-drive tugs was acquired, all of which were constructed by Bharati Shipyard Ltd, of Ratnagiri, to the south of Mumbai. The **Sudhirmulji** was one of these tugs and is seen here underway at Mumbai on 26 December 1999. She was completed in April 1998 and has a gross tonnage of 288. She is powered by two 6-cylinder Ulstein Bergen AS (Normo) diesels of 3580bhp driving a pair of Aquamaster US 1701/3000 azimuthing propulsion units, which give her a bollard pull of 50 tonnes and a service speed of 10 knots. All six tugs are fitted for fire-fighting and equipped for pollution control, and have fully air-conditioned accommodation for seven persons.

(Nigel Jones)

Santa Cruz is the principal port for the island of Tenerife in the Canaries, one of its major trades being the export of bananas. It is also an important ferry port, and can offer bunkering facilities to vessels requiring fuel. In more recent times it has also become an important destination for cruise ships. In 1991 the port was served by four tugs. CIRESA of Algeciras provided the 1982-built tugs **Algeciras** and **Coria**, whilst Compania Canaria de Remolques SA stationed the **Arucas** of 1974, and the **El Guanche** at the port. The **Arucas** had replaced the **Orotava** of 1970 at Santa Cruz by early 1990. On 15 March 1991 the **El Guanche** has just completed her duties, assisting with the sailing of a reefer, and is returning to her

berth. She was previously the **Torre Paloma** for Remolques de Malaga SA (REMASA) until 1983, and was constructed by Enrique y Cia. SA at Vigo in 1974. She was fitted for fire-fighting and was powered by a 6-cylinder MWM diesel of 2850bhp, built by Fabrica de San Carlos SA. Tug owner Compania Canaria de Remolques SA, also operated tugs from Las Palmas in Gran Canaria, and appears to have been taken over by the Boluda group by 1999. It is not known what has become of the **El Guanche** as by 2011 she no longer appeared in Lloyd's Register.

(Andrew Wiltshire)

The elderly tug **Bamse** is seen arriving at Turku on 18 June 2012 and has a lengthy history. She was completed in 1916 by Bergsunds Mekaniske Verksted A/B at Stockholm as the **Isbrytaren II** for Swedish shipowner Norrköpings Hamnstyrelse, of Norrköping. She had a gross tonnage of 220 and an overall length of 101 feet, and her main machinery consisted of a triple expansion steam engine built by the shipyard. It is known that she was renamed **Pampus** in 1953 and that in 1958 she passed to Oskarshamns Hamndirektion at Oskarshamn when she took the name **Björn**. In 1964 she became the **Akke** for Mattson Stevedoring Company of Kokkola, Finland and at this point became a motor tug. Her new main engine was an 8-cylinder Mak Maschinenbau GmbH of 1400bhp. In 1978 as the **Akke**, her overall length was increased to 103 feet and her grt was now recorded as 232. Remaining under the Finnish flag, she passed to Suomen Yritysrahoitus OY (Finska Foretags Finans AB) in 1983, and later to O/Y Yxpila Hinaus-Bogsering A/B also of Kokkola, in 1998. She became the **Bamse** in 2011 for Mattasnitty, of Parainen.

(K Brzoza)

The Republic of Cyprus is located in the eastern Mediterranean, and is an island that since 1974 has been politically divided. In the north is the Turkish occupied territory known as the Turkish Republic of Northern Cyprus and takes in the port of Famagusta, originally the major port for the island. A new port was constructed during 1971 at Limassol in the south, and since 1974 has become the main port for the island. Larnaca in the south-east of the island also plays an important role as since 1973 a new multi-purpose port facility has been in use. The Government of the Republic of Cyprus (Port Authority) operates four tugs, keeping three at the port of Limassol. The **Marion** was one of three new tugs built in India in the 1990s to update the fleet. She was new in 1994 along with her sister the **Prinias** and were completed in India by the Bharati Shipyard Ltd at Ratnagiri. At 338grt, these are large twin Voith Schneider tractor tugs with a bollard pull of 35 tonnes. Each tug is powered by a pair of 8-cylinder diesels by Ruston Diesels Ltd of 3480bhp and is fitted for fire-fighting. The third similar tug arrived in 1996 and is named **Aspelia**. The fourth tug in the fleet is the elderly 1300bhp **Othello** of 1966, which was built in the UK at Beverley. This nice view of the **Marion** was taken on 8 April 2002, when she was based at Larnaca.

(Roy Cressey collection)

The South African government (Railways and Harbours Administration) also operated a small fleet of rather splendid steam-powered pilot tugs. A total of ten were delivered between 1947 and 1959 and varied between 100 and 176 grt, and joined a handful of pre-war pilot tugs which included the *Ulundi* of 1927. No fewer than four different yards completed the post-war pilot tugs, with the final five being built in Venice in 1959. The subject of this photograph is the *S. G. Stephens*, one of a pair completed by Richard Dunston Ltd of Thorne near Goole in 1952, the sister tug being the *R. A. Leigh*. They were by far the largest of the pilot tugs at 176grt and both were twin-screw vessels. As built they had coal-fired boilers supplying steam to a pair of triple-expansion steam engines of 560ihp manufactured by McKie & Baxter Ltd giving them a speed of 10 knots. It is thought that both tugs were converted to oil-firing in the early 1970s. The *S. G. Stephens* was based at Cape Town and this is where we see her entering the Duncan dock in January 1977. After diesel powered pilot boats were introduced from the 1970s, the steam pilot tugs would often be used to assist smaller ships in port such as foreign trawlers. The *S. G. Stephens* was taken out of service by 1982, and after the sale to an Australian owner fell through, was soon broken up at Cape Town.

(Trevor Jones)

The *Ingénieur Reibell* dates from 1908, when she was completed as the *Sir Walter Raleigh* along with her sistership *Sir Francis Drake*, by Cammell Laird & Co Ltd at Birkenhead for the Great Western Railway Company. The *Sir Walter Raleigh* was a tender tug of 478grt and initially served at Fishguard before taking up duties at Plymouth. She was a twin-screw vessel of 1200ihp and had provision for 100 passengers. She operated for the Admiralty during both world wars and was damaged in an air raid at Plymouth in 1940. She returned to the Great Western Railway at the end of 1945, but in 1947 eventually passed to Overseas Towage and Salvage. In 1948 they resold her to French owners Société Cherbourgeoise de Remorquage & de Sauvetage at Cherbourg for further use as a tender. She was broken up at Le Havre in about 1968. In this view dating from June 1967 the *Ingénieur Reibell* is seen lying alongside the passenger ship *La Bretonnière* which dates from 1914 and was built by Nuscke & Co AG, Stettin-Grabow as the German *Grussgott* (781grt) for Norddeutscher Lloyd of Bremen. The vessels operated together at Cherbourg serving the large liners that anchored off the port, although the *La Bretonnière* was never classed as a tender tug.

(Derek Chaplin)

TUGS AT WORK By the mid-1950s many tug owners considered steam tugs uneconomical and outdated and some chose to motorise a number of them. This would very often lead to the tug having an extended life and the *St. Eval* is a very good example. She was delivered to Steel and Bennie Ltd, Glasgow, in April 1930 as the *Chieftain*, a tug of 196grt powered by a 830ihp 2-cylinder steam reciprocating engine. She was built on the Clyde by Scott and Sons of Bowling and was fitted with a new 8-cylinder Deutz engine of 660bhp in June 1957. Steel and Bennie converted two further steam tugs to motor, the *Warrior* in 1958 and *Cruiser* in 1963. The *Chieftain* was sold to Falmouth Towage Co Ltd in 1967 becoming the *St. Eval*, and in 1969 was re-engined once again. This time a 16-cylinder General Motors diesel made in 1944 and of 1460bhp was fitted and her gross tonnage changed to 209. Five years later on 6 August 1974, we see her at work on the River Fal. In 1987 the *St. Eval* was sold to De Savary, London, as an America's Cup support vessel, and in 1988/89 was converted to a yacht at Falmouth and classified as such. By 1992 she had crossed the Atlantic and was owned by Blueridge Investments Ltd (Fred Larsson) and registered in the Cayman Islands. Further conversion work was undertaken at Seattle on the west coast of the United States to enhance her standard of finish as a yacht. Still retaining her name *St. Eval*, she was later based at Vancouver and still existed in 2012.

(John Wiltshire)

Many of the Voith Schneider tractor tugs that were delivered new to the Rotterdam-based fleet of Nieuwe Rotterdamse Sleepdienst (NRS), went on to find new homes around the world. One such tug is the Portuguese-owned **Montebelo**, which dates from 1963. She was built by NV Scheepswerven HH Bodewes, Millingen a/d Rijn, in the Netherlands and launched as the **Panter**, but completed as the **Stroombank**. She was of 127grt with an overall length of 86 feet and a beam of 25 feet. She was fitted with twin Voith Schneider propulsion units driven by a pair of 8-cylinder Stork Ricardo diesels of 1220bhp. As the **Stroombank** she operated at Europoort initially for NRS, and then for Smit Habour Towage from 1988. She was later sold in 1999 to Straits Towage, Gibraltar, and became the **Straits II**. In 2002 she passed to Reboques e Assistencia Naval Ltd of Setubal, Portugal and became the **Montebelo**. This fleet came under the control of the Svitzer Group in 2004 and in 2011 her owner was quoted as Lisbontugs – Companhia de Rebocadores SA (Svitzer Europe Holding BV). In this view dated 28 August 2002, the **Montebelo** is busy in the docks at Lisbon.

(John Wiltshire)

The shipping company Em Z Svitzer hailing from Copenhagen in Denmark has been active for more than 175 years. They were early pioneers in the salvage industry, and eventually provided services around the world. In more recent times they have expanded greatly with the acquisition of many large tug operators both close to home and overseas, and they are serving more than thirty countries in 2013. The *Mimer*, purchased in 1974, was built in 1956 by Werft Schulte & Bruns of Emden as the *Norderney* for West German owner Ems Schlepper AG, Emden. She was 94 feet in length and had a 6-cylinder MWM diesel of 1080bhp. In 1970 the *Norderney* was sold to Norslep Bugser & Bjergningsselskap of Kristiansand and renamed *Rex*. In 1974 she was purchased by A/S Em Z Svitzer's Salvage Co Ltd and registered in Copenhagen as *Mimer*. The following year her original engine was replaced by a 12-cylinder Alpha diesel of 1740bhp, and was now coupled to a controllable-pitch propeller which gave her a speed of 10 knots. She is seen in the Queen Alexandra Dock at Cardiff on 28 June 1983, about to embark on a voyage with her tow. Svitzer sold the *Mimer* in 1985 to Norwegian owner I/S Robust (Peder Arnesen) of Farsund who renamed her *Tranevaag*. In 1987 she became the *Hadarvag* for Ulstein, of Aalesund, and in 2000 became the *Oyvag* working for Kvernhusvik Skipsverft AS of Melandsjø.

(John Wiltshire)

Construction of the Panama Canal was started by the French in 1881, but abandoned after eight years. The project was completed by the United States in 1913 as an elevated canal with man-made lakes with lock systems, and officially opened the following year. The territory it occupied became known as the Panama Canal Zone and was controlled by the United States until 1977. The Panama Canal Commission has operated a fleet of powerful tugs for many years to provide assistance to large vessels transiting the canal, although towage in the lock systems is taken care of by the shore mounted electric locomotives known as "mules". The twin-screw tug *Alianza* is seen at work on the canal assisting a cruise ship on 9 October 1999. She dates from 1981 and was built by the Bollinger Machine Shop & Shipyard Inc at Lockport, Louisiana along with the similar tug *Progreso*. The *Alianza* had a grt of 347 and was powered by two 12-cylinder General Motors Electro-Motive diesels of 3000bhp giving her a bollard pull of 36 tonnes. In 2013 the Panama Canal was in the process of taking delivery of fourteen new tugs, and will eventually operate a fleet of forty-four vessels.

(Harry Cutter)

On 4 May 1979 the small Turkish steam tug *Liman 2* (abbreviated to *L.2* on the vessel), is seen making her way through the Bosphorus near Istanbul with a tow. She was built in the Netherlands by L A Kreber of Vlaardingen in 1936 for the Istanbul Port Company, and was deployed as a harbour tug at Istanbul as well as undertaking short tows on the Bosphorus. The *Liman 2* is a vessel of 62 feet overall length with a gross tonnage of just 50. She has a triple expansion engine of 170ihp, and relies on a single-flue coal-fired Scotch boiler to supply her steam.

She continued to work commercially until 1988, and in 1990 she was purchased by a Mr Rahmi M Koc who set about restoring her to full working order, a task which was completed in July 1992. The *Liman 2* is now a working exhibit at the Rahmi M Koc Museum in Istanbul, and regularly offers short cruises to the public at the Golden Horn in the summer months.

(John Wiltshire)

The steam tug **Cervia** was a very late example of a Foremost class Empire-type tug being completed on 30 April 1946 by Alexander Hall & Co Ltd, Aberdeen as **Empire Raymond** for the Ministry of War Transport. As such she passed to William Watkins Ltd, London, the following month gaining the name **Cervia** in April 1947. With a gross tonnage of 233, she was an oil-fired tug from new and had a triple expansion engine of 700ihp built by the shipyard. In 1950 she was put under the management of Ship Towage (London) Ltd, and on 25 October 1954 capsized and sank while towing the **Arcadia** at Tilbury, with the loss of five lives. The **Cervia** was raised three days later and eventually returned to service on the Thames. In September 1968 her owners became London Tugs Limited and she continued to earn her keep until June 1971 when she was laid up. In this view towards the end of her career on the Thames, she is seen at work off the Royal Docks in January 1970. In March 1972 the **Cervia** passed to Michael List-Brain and Martin Stevens for inclusion in a proposed Medway Maritime Museum. This failed to materialise and she was put back into commercial service with ITL International Towing Ltd of Sittingbourne, and could often be found around the UK on coastal towing duties. The **Cervia** was eventually put on loan to the East Kent Maritime Museum in 1985 and moved to a permanent base at Ramsgate. She remains there in 2013 having been partly restored.

(the late C C Beazley)

Solent Towage is a subsidiary of Ostensjö Rederi AS, and provides tug and tanker escort services at the Esso Fawley Marine Terminal on the Solent near Southampton. Solent Towage took over operations from the Red Funnel Group in 1994 with two large purpose-built tugs the **Silex** and **Thrax**, and has continued to provide modern tugs at this terminal ever since. In 2006 the first of three large Voith Schneider tractor tugs, the **Tenax** was delivered, followed by the **Phenix** in 2007 and the **Apex** in 2008. The **Apex** has a gross tonnage of 643 and was built by Astilleros Gondan SA of Castropol in northern Spain.

She is powered by two 8-cylinder Rolls Royce Bergen diesels of 6852bhp driving a pair of Voith Schneider propulsion units, and giving an impressive bollard pull in the region of 67 tonnes. The **Apex** is equiped for fire-fighting and pollution control and rather interestingly has six cabins for passengers. We see her at work off Calshot in this view dated 15 March 2009. In 2011 her registered owner was given as Boreas Shipping Ltd, Southampton.

(Douglas Cromby)

In Morocco tugs can be found working at many ports including Casablanca, Rabat, Agadir, Tangier and Mohammedia, and some of these will belong to government-operated fleets. Société Chérifienne de Remorquage & d'Assistance has maintained a tug fleet for many years, and at one time included three Empire-type steam tugs, as well as another steam tug, the **Moulay Idriss** which they received new in 1952. France had interests in Morocco, but after 1956 the country gained its independence. Even so, at least four former French Les Abeille tugs found service with Société Chérifienne de Remorquage & d'Assistance joining the fleet between 1978 and 1982. The **El Hafid** was a single-screw motor tug that was purchased new in 1982. She had been constructed in the Netherlands by Scheepswerf "De Waal" BV at Zaltbommel and had a grt of 248. The **El Hafid** had an overall length of 107 feet and was fitted for fire-fighting. Her main engine was a Deutz of 2799bhp. In this photograph she is seen working at Casablanca in August 1990. In 2007 she passed to Action Shipping of Casablanca and was renamed **Zamoura**. By 2013 the fleet was operating modern Damen Stan tugs such as the **El Beida** and **Sidi Moussa**.

(Brian Fisher)

Mozambique is a country in south-east Africa which established independence from Portuguese rule in 1975. At this point the port and capital city Lourenco Marques became known as Maputo. A number of steam tugs were in service at Maputo, but these were gradually replaced by motor tugs including a pair purchased from the South African government. The **Lucheringo** was one of a pair of twin-screw tugs completed in 1980 for Government of the People's Republic of Mozambique, her sister being the **Messalo**. These tugs were built in the Netherlands by BV Schps v/h HH Bodewes at Millingen and the **Lucheringo** had a gross tonnage of 222 and an overall length of 93 feet. Her main engines were two 6-cylinder Stork-Werkspoor B. which developed a total of 2300bhp. This view of the **Lucheringo** attending a bulk carrier at Maputo dates from 10 April 1988. Mozambique was blighted by civil war for many years and investment on port infrastructure was virtually non-existent. The two remaining operational harbour tugs at Maputo were considered unreliable and underpowered, resulting in a number of incidents. In 2003 a pair of modern Z-Peller tugs dating from 1989 was acquired from Hong Kong Towage and Salvage, and took the names **Polana** and **Xefina**.

(Andrew Wiltshire collection)

The Spanish tug **Marbella** is seen hard at work manoeuvring a bulk carrier at Malaga on 21 September 1990. At this time Malaga was served by four ship-handling tugs, the **Torre del Mar** (1966) and **Torre Vigia** (1982) operating for Remolques de Malaga SA (REMASA), and the identical tugs **Marbella** and **Fuengirola** which were owned by Maritima Espimunos SA. The latter pair were named after small coastal towns on the Costa del Sol near Malaga, and were delivered in early 1975 from the shipbuilder Ast De Santander SA at Santander. Each tug had a gross tonnage of 141, an overall length of 96 feet and a breadth of 25 feet, and they were equipped for fire-fighting. Main machinery consisted of a pair of 12-cylinder Baudouin diesel engines built under licence by Internacional Diesel SA , coupled to a controllable-pitch propeller which gave the tugs a speed of 12 knots. In 2006 the **Marbella** passed to Remolques Unidos and was transferred to Santander, and in 2009 was sold to Italian owners Silem SRL. Now renamed **Tico** she is currently based at the port of Villa San Giovanni. Her sister **Fuengirola** passed to Nigerian interests in 2008 eventually taking the name **Ocean Wave**.

(Andrew Wiltshire)

The USSR continued to use steam tugs after World War Two, and had many new examples completed at its own yards right up until the end of the 1950s. Others steam tugs were completed in Finland, Poland and China. Details of these vessels and their ultimate fate can be somewhat patchy, but we do know a little about this fine-looking steam tug, the *Primorsk* of 1957, which is seen working at Kronstadt near Leningrad (now St Petersburg) on 15 June 1978. She had an overall length of 107 feet and a breadth of 26 feet and her main machinery consisted of a 480ihp triple expansion steam engine which gave her a speed in the region of 10.5 knots. The *Primorsk* was one of a class of at least sixty similar tugs built between 1948 and 1958 by the Petrozavod shipyard in Leningrad, and most had a gross tonnage of around 239. They were distributed across the whole of the Soviet Union with examples to be found working anywhere from the Black Sea to the Barentsz Sea and the Baltic ports, and a number were also deployed in the naval dockyards. At least four were known to be active in the Leningrad area in 1978 often supplying steam as well as performing towing. It would seem that most of these tugs had been scrapped by the end of the 1990s, but a number survived including the *Rudokop* also of 1957. This tug was purchased by Thordon Bearings of Canada in 1990 and visited many countries as a publicity vessel. In 2008 the *Rudokop* still survived in a semi-preserved state with a Norwegian owner.

(John Wiltshire)

Towage in the port of Brisbane from 1948/49 was undertaken by William & Co Pty Ltd using the steam tugs *Fearless* (1895), *Forceful* (1925), *Carlock* (1929) and *Coringa*, the former *Empire Peggy* of 1945. The *Fearless* was scrapped in 1952 and a replacement tug bearing the same name entered the fleet in 1954. She was an oil-fired vessel of 249grt that had been built in 1945 by Midland Shipyards Ltd of Midland, Ontario, as the *Rockwing* for the Canadian government, and was one of a class of eighteen similar steam tugs. Her machinery consisted of a 1000ihp triple-expansion steam engine built by Collingwood Shipyards Ltd. By 1946 she was operating for the British government at Hong Kong, and in 1948 became the *Tapline 2* for the Overseas Petroleum Co of London. In 1949 she was sold to Arabian American Oil Co Ltd of Saudi Arabia and renamed *Abqaiq 3*. By 1965 the four steam tugs at Brisbane were working for the Queensland Tug Co Pty Ltd, and the *Fearless* of 1945 is seen here in the early 1960s on the Brisbane River. She was withdrawn from service in 1972 and sold to Keith Le Leu who took her to Adelaide where she was donated to the South Australian Maritime Museum. In 1982 the *Fearless* was hauled onto the banks of the Port River close to Birkenhead Bridge and has occupied this spot ever since. Meanwhile back in Brisbane, the 1925-built *Forceful* survives as a working exhibit for the Queensland Maritime Museum.

(World Ship Society collection)

The Israel Ports Authority was established on 1 July 1961 and early examples of tugs operated included the UK-built steam tugs *Eytanah* of 1930, *Tzuriyah* of 1935 and the locally-built motor tug *Uzziyah* of 1961. In July 1998 the Israel Railways merged with the Ports Authority to form the Israel Ports and Railway Authority which now serves the ports of Haifa, Ashdod and Eilat. In this view we see the *Gaash* assisting the Bulgarian-flagged bulk carrier *Ograjden* at Ashdod on 22 October 1996. She is one of two identical Voith tractor tugs to enter service with the Israel Ports Authority in 1993, doing so shortly after her sister the *Saar II*. The *Gaash* was completed by Israel Shipyards Ltd at Haifa and has a gross tonnage of 267. Power for her twin Voith Schneider propulsion units is provided by a pair of 6-cylinder MWM (Deutz) diesels of 2876bhp, which give her a speed of 12 knots. The *Gaash* is fitted for fire-fighting and her current owner is named as Ashdod Port Co Ltd, Ashdod.

(Jim McFaul)

The **Mayfield** is a large twin-unit Voith Schneider tractor that works at the Australian port of Newcastle, New South Wales, located at the mouth of the Hunter River. She is one of three identical sisterships at this port that have an interesting history. The **Mayfield** was built in 1990 as **Radhwa 19** for the State Company for Oil Projects (SCOP), Iraq, her sisters being the **Radhwa 18** and **Radhwa 20**. Her hull was constructed in the Netherlands by Scheepsbouw Alblas B. and she was completed by BV Scheepswerf Damen of Gorinchem. They are fire-fighting tugs of 496grt powered by two 18-cylinder MAN vee-type diesels of 4894bhp giving a bollard pull of 48 tonnes. On delivery to Iraq all three tugs were laid up at Malta due to the bankruptcy of the customer. In 1993 they were sold to Hunter Towage Services, Newcastle (managed by BHP Transport Pty Ltd), and **Radhwa 19** carried the name **R-19** for the duration of the delivery voyage. All three tugs soon entered service and were named **Mayfield**, **Carrington** and **Wickham**. In 2004 ownership passed to Adsteam Harbour Pty Ltd, and this is how we see the **Mayfield** at work in Adsteam colours on 16 January 2005. By 2006 she was managed by Svitzer Australasia Pty Ltd, and in 2007 all three tugs passed to Svitzer SPCZ Pty Ltd, Newcastle. The **Mayfield** was still at work in 2013.

(Roy Cressey collection)

The final pair of Empire-type steam tugs to remain operational in the Bristol Channel could be found working at Avonmouth in the fleet of C J King and Sons (Tugs) Ltd. These were the *Sea Alarm* of 1941 and the *Sea Queen* of 1944. The latter was an oil-fired tug built by Henry Scarr at Hessle, but the *Sea Alarm* was to be the last coal-fired steam tug to be engaged in ship-handling in the Bristol Channel, and as such would often sail to the South Wales port of Barry to replenish her coal bunker. The *Sea Alarm* was a Warrior-class Empire-tug launched on 13 August 1941 by the shipyard of J Crown and Sons Ltd, Sunderland, and completed in the following October with a gross tonnage of 263. Her triple expansion was supplied by Swan Hunter and Wigham Richardson and

was recorded with an output of 1000ihp. From completion she was owned by the Ministry of War Transport and based on the Clyde managed by Clyde Shipping Co Ltd, Glasgow, to whom she passed in 1946 as the *Flying Fulmar*. Ten years later Bristol became her home port when she was purchased by the Alarm Steam Tug Co Ltd (C J King & Sons (Tugs) Ltd) and given the new name *Sea Alarm*. She was taken out of service in 1972 and sold in early 1973 to T W Ward Ltd, Briton Ferry, for scrap. However, she was reprieved and passed to the Welsh Industrial and Maritime Museum, and quickly moved to Cardiff. She was broken up at Cardiff in 1998 to make way for the redevelopment of Cardiff Bay.

(John Wiltshire)

TOWAGE IN NORTH AMERICAN WATERS A total of four similar USMC V-tug type V2-ME-A1 tugs were completed at the shipyard of Canulette Shipbuilding Co, Slidell, Louisiana. One of these was the ***Port Vincent*** which was delivered to the US Maritime Commission at Slidell in May 1943. She had a gross tonnage of 196, an overall length of 94 feet and was powered by a 4-stroke Enterprise Engine & Foundry Co diesel engine of 1000bhp. In 1946 the ***Port Vincent*** was sold to the Standard Oil Co of California as the ***Standard No. 3*** and registered at San Francisco, and was put to service at Puget Sound. After a very impressive length of service as the ***Standard No. 3***, a change came in 1993 when she passed to Donald J House of Juneau, Alaska, and reverted to her original name ***Port Vincent***. A further change occurred in 1996 when she passed to Tyee Maritime Inc at Sitka as ***Thunderbird***, and she remained in service under this name with this owner in 2012. We see her on 20 May 1989 at Seattle as ***Standard No. 3***.

(Rick Garcia)

The Sept-Isles iron ore terminal receives ore by rail from the Iron Ore Company of Canada mines at Labrador City, and from Sept Isles it is shipped to destinations around the world. Working at this terminal is the 396grt tug **Pointe Aux Basques** which in this view is operating for Eastern Canada Towing Ltd. She was completed on 30 November 1972 for Mil Tug & Salvage Ltd, Halifax, which then became Eastern Canada Towing Ltd on 1 January 1973. She was built at Collingwood Shipyards Ltd, Collingwood and was followed into service by the sister tug **Pointe Marguerite**. The **Pointe Aux Basques** is a powerful twin-screw tug with a maximum bollard pull of 73 tonnes, and is powered by two 12-cylinder GMC diesels developing 5400bhp and driving two fixed-pitch propellers in steerable Kort nozzles. Tragically in November 1978, the **Pointe Marguerite** was badly damaged in a collision and sank, but her sister still survives in service in 2013. In 1989 Eastern Canada Towage became a wholly-owned subsidiary of Cory Towage Ltd, which passed to the Svitzer group with the ownership of **Pointe Aux Basques** becoming Svitzer Canada Ltd, Halifax. She was idle after Svitzer's contract with Iron Ore Canada at Sept-Iles ended on 1 August 2013 and later in the year it was reported that she had been sold to Groupe Ocean and renamed **Ocean Basques**.

(René Beauchamp)

Foss Maritime can trace its roots back to 1889 when it was founded by Thea Foss in Tacoma as a rowboat business. By 1916 it was trading as Foss Launch and Tug Company and by 1930 its fleet was diesel powered. Today Foss is one of the largest tug operators on the west coast of the United States. The subject of this photograph is the **Peter Foss** of 1978, and she is seen underway at Long Beach, California, on 17 May 1999. She is one of a class of five similar tugs completed by Main Iron Works Inc at Houma, and should not be confused with another tug in this series that was launched as **Peter Foss** in 1977, but completed as **Moana Hele** for service in Hawaii. The 1978-built vessel was delivered to Foss Launch and Tug Co Ltd at Seattle in February 1978, and is a 2250bhp twin-screw ship powered by a pair of 16-cylinder Caterpillar diesels. In 1999 the **Peter Foss** was one of two conventional tugs converted to an azimuthing stern-drive (ASD) type tug by Marine Industries at Seattle. She received new Caterpillar engines with a total output of 3300bhp which increased her bollard pull by 63% and considerably improved her manoeuvrability. In May 2004 she was sold to Sort Well Inc, of Oakland, and renamed **Liberty**, and can now be found working at Portland, Los Angles and Oakland.

(Nigel Jones)

McAllister Towing and Transportation is another large tug operator in the United States with a history going back nearly 150 years. In 2013 they operated around seventy tugs and served seventeen locations on the east coast of the United States. The subject of this photograph is the **McAllister Boys** of 1966, the second motor tug to carry this name. She was constructed by McDermott Shipyards at Morgan City, Louisiana, as **El Buey Grande** for Tidewater Marine of New Orleans. She is 199 gross tons and is a twin-screw tug powered by a pair of 16-cylinder 2-stroke General Motors diesels of 3600bhp. In 1991 she briefly became **Denise D. Defelice** for Defelice Marine Towing, Lake Charles, which was taken over by Gulf Fleet. Later in 1991 she was renamed **Enforcer** for Jore Corporation of Seattle, before passing to McAllister in 2001. The **McAllister Boys** is 122 feet overall length, with a double-drum towing winch and equipped with three fire-fighting monitors. In 2012 she remains in service as the **McAllister Boys** with her owner being described as McAllister Towing & Transportataion Co Inc (MT&T) of New York.

(Marc Piché)

The history of Moran Towing can be traced back to 1855, and the company has grown to become the largest providing towage on the east coast of the United States. Steam tugs were gradually phased out from the 1930s and after World War Two it began to acquire other tug operators, and remained a family concern until 1994. The **Kerry Moran** was built at the Jakobson Shipyard Inc Oyster Bay in 1963 with a gross tonnage of 289. She was a diesel-electric tug that had two previously used General Motors diesel engines driving generators. These supplied power to a pair of electric motors geared to a single propeller shaft. The **Kerry Moran** was delivered new to Tug E F Moran Jr Inc Wilmington, and followed her sistership **Patricia Moran** of 1962 into service. In this view in March 1992, she is seen working at New York. Both the **Patricia Moran** and **Kerry Moran** were given a new lease of life in 1999. They were taken to the yard of Hendry at Tampa and converted into stern-drive tugs, both featuring a pair of Ulstein propulsion units. Both tugs received a new pair of GMC-EMD diesels of total output 4200bhp, and also had their accommodation substantially rebuilt to give the vessels a much more modern and practical appearance.

(Paul Andow)

The **Pacific Escort** is an example of a US Army design 377-A tug, and is thought to be one of eighteen such vessels built. She was completed in April 1944 for the US Army as **LT-535** at the yard of Levingston Shipbuilding at Orange, Texas. She was 143 feet in length with a gross tonnage of about 561 tons. Her propulsion was by way of diesel-electric means, with a pair of 12-cylinder General Motors diesels of 1900bhp as prime movers for two generators. Two electric motors were then geared to a single shaft resulting in a service speed of 11.5 knots. The **LT-535** was acquired by the United States Navy in 1985 and named **Pacific Escort**. Her intended use was as an escort for submarines, but she also had a role as an oceanographic research ship and she was based at Mare Island Naval Shipyard in California. This is how we see her, from the Golden Gate Bridge, outbound from San Francisco, in May 1986. Despite her age, she found further service from 1996 after the US Navy had finished with her. She became the **Ataboy** for Dana Marine Services, Orange and in 1998 she ceased to be a diesel-electric tug, upon receiving new GM engines coupled to a conventional transmission. By now the tug had a revised gross tonnage of 496 and total power output of 3800bhp. In 2010 she was working for Nigerian owner Hansen Dreijer Marine as **Brittania U III**.

(Ray Thorsteinson)

TUGS IN AUSTRALASIA Hobart is the largest port on the island of Tasmania located off the south-east tip of Australia. The Australian tug *Cape Forestier* is seen underway on an incredibly flat sea off Hobart on 29 March 1983. She was built in 1936 by Cockatoo Docks & Eng Co Pty Ltd at Sydney as the steam tug *Warang* for Waratah Tug & Salvage Co Pty Ltd, and based in Sydney. She was 102 feet in length and was fitted with a triple expansion steam engine of 540ihp made by Muir & Houston Ltd in 1909, and supplied with steam from a coal-fired boiler. In 1970 she was converted to a motor tug and fitted with two 16-cylinder General Motors diesels made way back in 1945. They were geared to a single propeller-shaft with a controllable-pitch propeller. She now had a grt of 218, and

in 1974 was sold to North Western Shipping and Towage Co Pty Ltd, (Hobart Tug and Lighterage Co Pty Ltd) Hobart, and renamed *Cape Forestier*. As such she was employed towing newsprint barges down the Derwent River to Hobart along with the tug *Cape Bruny* of 1949, until that service eventually finished. The *Cape Forestier* was partly dismantled in the early 1990s at Launceston, with many parts going to Australian Maritime College for training purposes. Her wheelhouse survives with the George Town and District Historical Society. Her hulk survives at Launceston, as does that of *Cape Bruny* together with some former newsprint barges.

(Andrew Wiltshire collection)

The Waratah Tug and Salvage Co was established in 1931 by the Adelaide Steamship Company and took over the operations of J and A Brown who were based at Sydney and Newcastle at the time. A large fleet of steam tugs was owned and included six British-built former Admiralty Saint-class tugs dating from 1919/20. Three tugs were purchased new, the last of which was the **Woona** delivered in 1954 by James Lamont of Port Glasgow, while the first motor tug **Wooree** arrived in 1958 from the British yard of Mitchison at Gateshead. She was followed in August 1959 by the subject of our photograph, the **Warilla** which at 208grt and 106 feet overall length, was of very similar proportions to the **Wooree**, and featured a hydroconic hull. However, the **Warilla** was built in Australia by Adelaide Ship Construction Ltd, of Adelaide, together with the very similar tugs **Kurnell** and **Walana** that went to other Australian fleets. The **Warilla** was powered by a 1040bhp engine manufactured by National Gas & Oil Engine Co Ltd and had a speed of 11.5 knots. In 1977 she was sold by Waratah Tug and Salvage Co Pty Ltd to Bettina Alder of Sydney and later towed to Singapore. By 1978 she was with Corfu Shipping Ltd under the Cypriot flag and in 1980 became the **Leros** for Archirodon Construction Co (Architug Shipping SA), Piraeus, and sailing under the Honduran flag. Her ultimate fate is unknown. She is seen underway at Newcastle, New South Wales, on 19 March 1966.

(John Mathieson [Russell Priest collection])

The Union Steamship Company Ltd of New Zealand was founded in Dunedin in 1875. It was acquired by P&O in 1917 but retained its identity and continued to trade until 2000. Two virtually identical Empire-type steam tugs the **Taioma** and **Tapuhi** were acquired in 1947 for use at the port of Welllington. They were examples of the Foremost class design, all eighteen of which were completed by Alexander Hall & Co Ltd of Aberdeen between 1942 and 1946. The **Taioma** was launched on 25 April 1944 as **Empire Jane** for the Ministry of War Transport and initially used for coastal towing until her arrival at Bombay in 1946. She moved to Singapore in 1947 and, along with the **Empire Shirley**, was sold to Union SS Co Ltd, becoming the **Taioma** and **Tapuhi**, respectively. The **Taioma** was an oil-fired steam tug powered by a 900ihp triple expansion engine which gave her a speed of 10 knots. We see her at work at Wellington in this view from the 1960s. The **Taioma** was withdrawn from service in 1971 and eventually sold in 1975 to Singapore owners but managed by Union SS Co Ltd. She was sold again in July 1978 and towed to Tauranga. Having been donated to the Tauranga District Museum, the **Taioma** was taken 4.5 miles over land to her new resting place. In 2000 the museum closed and the tug was taken back to the coast where she was scuttled as an artificial reef near Motiti Island, Mount Manganui.

(World Ship Society collection)

The port of Bluff is located near the city of Invercargill on New Zealand's South Island. Originally the port was operated by the Bluff Harbour Board which in 1958 became the Southland Harbour Board. The well-known steam tug **Awarua** of 1932 provided towage at the port for many years until the arrival of the first large motor tug, the **Hauroko**, in 1968. She was a Voith Schneider tractor built by Whangarei Engineering and Construction Co Ltd, at Whangarei, North Island, and was followed in 1973 by the slightly larger **Monowai**. At 303grt, the **Monowai** is an impressive tug that has been equipped for fire-fighting as well as having basic salvage facilities. She is powered by two 6-cylinder Ruston Paxman (English Electric) diesel engines which develop 2682bhp and drive two Voith Schneider cycloidal propellers giving the tug a bollard pull of about 30 tonnes. In 1988 the **Monowai** passed to South Port NZ Ltd, which succeeded the Southland Harbour Board after privatisation. A third new tractor tug, the **Awanui** of 1988, was purchased in 2000 from the Northland Port Corporation (NZ) Ltd of Whangerei, becoming the **Hauroko** having replaced the 1968-built tug of that name. The **Monowai** remains in active service in 2013. She is seen on 17 August 2009.

(Chris Howell)

Papua New Guinea lies to the north-east of the Australian mainland and is separated by the Arafura Sea and the Coral Sea. Pacific Towing PNG Ltd was established in 1977 to provide towage in that country and in 2013 operated a fleet of eleven tugs serving nine ports including Port Moresby, Lae, Madang and Oro Bay. Delivered new in 1982 was the twin-screw tug *Pacific Gulf* which we see here in her first year of service at Port Moresby on 22 December 1982. She was completed at Singapore by the Pan Asia Shipyard and Engineering Co Pte Ltd with a gross tonnage of 103. Her hull dimensions are 70 feet overall length with a breadth of 22 feet. She has a bollard pull of 12 tonnes provided by two Caterpillar D3048TA diesels of 730bhp, driving a pair of 1.67m diameter fixed-pitch propellers in nozzles. The *Pacific Gulf* has accommodation for eight persons, and it was claimed she was capable of steaming for twenty-one days at full power. In late 2011 she was renamed *Iamelele* after a volcano in Seymour Bay, Papua New Guinea.

(Jeff Screeton)

The **Aucklander** was a steam tug that was launched in November 1957 by Fleming & Ferguson Ltd, of Paisley, on the River Clyde. She was the last tug to be built at this yard which closed in 1969. The **Aucklander** was delivered in March 1958 to her owners the Auckland Harbour Board at Auckland on New Zealand's North Island, and entered service alongside the Harbour Boards other steam tugs, the **William C. Daldy** of 1935 (now preserved), and the **Te Awhina** of 1908. The **Aucklander** had a grt of 454 and was a large tug with an overall length of 129 feet. She had a speed of 10 knots and was of twin-screw layout, being powered by two triple expansion steam engines of 1762ihp. This view of the **Aucklander** at work dates from 1981, and five years later she was sold to businessman Clem Griffiths for use as a floating restaurant at Wellington and renamed **Tapuhi II**. By 1992 her machinery had been removed and the conversion was soon completed. The restaurant known as the *Tug on the Bay* subsequently opened in 1994 at Oriental Bay in Wellington and still exists in 2013. Auckland Harbour Board subsequently purchased modern Voith Schneider tractor tugs, and operates in 2013 as Ports of Auckland Ltd.

(Chris Howell)

As steam tugs go, the **Wyola** was rather unusual in that she had two funnels, a feature that made her rather distinctive and was necessary because of her two front-to-front boilers. She was quite an elderly tug too, being completed in July 1912 for The Swan River Shipping Co Ltd of Fremantle in Western Australia. Her builder was J T Eltringham & Co, of South Shields, a company well-known for building many fine tugs, but which went out of business in 1922. The **Wyola** was a coal-fired vessel powered by an 1100ihp triple-expansion steam engine and had a gross tonnage of 306. She was 132 feet in length, but her beam was only 24 feet. Her delivery voyage to Australia is well-documented, and took her via Gibraltar, Ceylon and Singapore, finally arriving at Fremantle on 5 October 1912. Just six years later she was requisitioned by Admiralty from 1918-20 and based at Malta as a rescue tug and formed part of the Mediterranean fleet. Upon returning to Australia her working life continued for another fifty years, her appearance changing very little in that time. This view of the **Wyola** was taken at Inner Harbour, Fremantle on 12 March 1969; her working days are nearly over. She was taken out of service on 10 January 1970 and immediately sold for scrap. The **Wyola** was taken to Robb Jetty in Cockburn Sound and beached. As recently as 2012 part of her keel and stern post remained partially buried in the sand.

(Ted Drake [Russell Priest collection])

TUGS SERVING LARGE PORTS The tug company NV Nieuwe Rotterdamse Sleepdienst was set up in 1960 by L Smit and Co of Rotterdam to provide towage at the new port facility Europoort. For this, two new diesel-electric tugs the **Steenbank** and **Schouwenbank** were delivered that year, followed in 1961 by the first of many Voith-Schneider tractors. Two conventional-propulsion tugs, the **Maasbank** and the **Vikingbank** arrived in 1965, from the shipyard of NV Schpswerven. v/h H H Bodewes, Millingen a/d Rijn, and were vessels of 227 grt with an overall length of 107 feet. They were each fitted with two 8-cylinder Stork-Ricardo diesels of 1320bhp, geared to a single propeller turning in a Kort nozzle.

The **Vikingbank** stranded in March 1967 and was declared a loss, but the **Maasbank** continued to serve Europoort, and also undertook offshore work in the North Sea. In 1977 she was sold to Nieuwe Vlissinge Sleepdienst NV of Flushing and renamed **Banckert**. In 1981 she passed to Van den Akker BV, also at Flushing, and in 1988 took the name **Takavar** under the Iranian flag for service with Iranian Marine Services (Smit-Tak) at Bandar Khomeini. As such she is known to have sunk in 1991. This view of the **Maasbank** dates from July 1974.

(the late C C Beazley)

Alexandria is the second largest city in Egypt and is a major seaport. It is thought to be one of the oldest ports in the world and in more recent times the Western Harbour has been the main commercial port. A new facility to ease congestion, the port of Dekhaila, opened at Alexandria in 1986. The Alexandria Port Authority took delivery of six new twin-screw tugs in 1978/79, four of which were named **Obour**, **Ramadan**, **Zamzam** and **October**. They were all completed in Japan by Towa Zosen KK at Shimonoseki and were all approximately 199grt. The **Zamzam** is seen underway at Alexandria passing a variety of shipping on 17 February 1996. She was completed in 1979 and is powered by two Yanmar 6GL-DT diesels with a combined output of 1598bhp. In 2010, the port authority received four new Voith Schneider tractor tugs each with a bollard pull of 55 tonnes. Meanwhile in 2011, the **Zamzam** was reported to be still in service.

(John Wiltshire)

Singapore is an island city-state in south-east Asia and gained its independence from Great Britain in 1963. Since then it has become a major financial centre and is one of the five busiest ports in the world. The Singapore Harbour Board was formed in 1912 and operated a small number of tugs including the steam tugs **Pitho** of 1914 and **Tunda** of 1928. In 1956 a new motor tug named **Tunda** was constructed at the Harbour Board's own yard, the Dockyard and Shiprepair Agency. She was a twin-screw tug of 152grt, with an overall length of 99 feet and was powered by a pair of Lister Blackstone diesels. Three similar vessels later appeared from the same yard. These were the **Tegoh** (1960), **Tambat** (1961) and **Tegap** (1962) and had a gross tonnage in the region of 160, but were shorter at 92 feet overall length. The Singapore Harbour Board was taken over by the newly created Port of Singapore Authority (PSA) in 1964, and soon introduced a three-shift system of cargo-handling, earning itself the reputation of "the port that never sleeps". This view of the **Tambat** was taken in March 1983, and her hull is starting to show signs of neglect. From 1972 many modern, powerful tugs were acquired, and by 2013 a fleet of around fifty ASD and tractor tugs was in service at Singapore.

(Frank Miles [Marc Piché collection])

French tug operator Cie Chambon Société Générale de Remorquage et de Travaux Maritimes was based at Marseille and many steam tugs were owned over the years. Later a base was also established at Sète. Motor tugs began to appear from 1948; by 1965 around fifteen tugs were operating at Marseille. One of the larger examples was the **Laurent Chambon** of 1960, a tug built in the Netherlands by NV Scheepswerf & GHBW. v/h Jonker & Stans at Hendrik-Ido-Ambacht. The **Laurent Chambon** had a gross tonnage 263 and was 109 feet overall length with a breadth of 27 feet and had a service speed of 12.5 knots. Her main engine was a little more unusual being a 1320bhp diesel manufactured by Swiss Locomotive & Machine Works. Here we see her at Marseille in June 1980, and by 1986 the official title of her registered owner was given as Compagnie Chambon, Marseille. In 1987 the **Laurent Chambon** was sold to Greek owners and became **Spiros Lekkas** for Portolos Salvage SA, Piraeus. By 2005 she was out of use and was still believed to be in lay-up in 2010, with her owners involved in a legal dispute, and as far as is known, she still exists in 2013. Returning to the port of Marseille, in 2011 Boluda France was the main provider of towage at the port.

(Andrew Wiltshire collection)

Crowley Marine Services can trace its roots back to 1892 in the San Francisco area and entered into tugboat operation in 1908. The rival towage company, Shipowners and Merchants Tugboat Company "Red Stack Tugs" was acquired by 1915. The business continued to expand and operations diversified into other areas of shipping and transportation. In 1952 two motor tugs, the **Sea Duke** and **Sea Scout**, were delivered to Crowley from the yard of Pacific Coast Engineering Co, Alameda in California. In this view taken at San Francisco in March 1989, the **Sea Scout** is clearly still very active some thirty-seven years later. She is a tug of 184grt and has an overall length of just less than 93 feet. Her main engine is a 12-cylinder 2-stroke General Motors diesel of 1000bhp, which was actually nine years older than the **Sea Scout** herself. By 1966 her registered owner within the Crowley organisation was described as Shipowners and Merchants Towboat Co Ltd at San Francisco. She was sold by Crowley in 2004 to Brusco Tug and Barge of Freeland and took the new name **Arcturus**. In 2013 Crowley Marine Services continued to operate tugs with a modern fleet serving the ports of San Fransisco, Los Angeles, San Diego, Long Beach and tugs are also to be found working in Alaska.

(Paul Andow)

It is thought that the Port of Antwerp Authority began operating its own fleet of tugs over one hundred years ago for service within the enclosed dock system. The Voith Schneider tractor tug has become the standard vessel since it first appeared at Antwerp in 1958. Five similar tugs were delivered by the St. Peter shipyard at Hemiksem and were numbered *62*, *43* to *46* and entered service between 1959 and 1962. In 1964, numbers *43* to *46* became *63* to *66* and it is thought that the subject of this photograph *64* (formerly *44*) built in 1959, did not actually enter service until November 1961. She is seen in action at Antwerp on a fine 19 August 1989. The tug was powered by a pair of ABC diesels with a combined output of 1120bhp driving a pair of Voith Schneider propulsion units which gave her a bollard pull of about 14 tonnes. Number *64* was refurbished in the mid-1980s eventually returning to service in March 1988, but was retired by 2007 when she was broken up locally at Hoboken. *62* and *65* were also scrapped, but *63* and *66* remain in service with the Belgian Navy as *Wasp* (A952) and *Ant* (A955) respectively.

(John Wiltshire)

The South African government (Railways and Harbours Administration), later restyled South African Transport Services, began introducing modern diesel tractor tugs in 1974 when it received four Voith Schneider-propelled vessels which included the **Jan Haywood** and **R. H. Tarpey**. All were built at Durban and had a bollard pull of 42 tonnes. In 1977/78 four Z-Peller-type stern drive tugs arrived followed by a further quartet of Voith tractors in 1980. The **Otto Buhr** was delivered in 1982 to South African Transport Services, and was a Schottel-type tractor tug of 295grt constructed at Durban by Dorman Long Vanderbijl Corp. (Dorbyl) Ltd. The **Otto Buhr** had twin Schottel SRP 1100 units driven by a pair of 6-cylinder Krupp Mak diesels of 3000bhp which produced a bollard pull of around 39 tonnes. In all six tugs of this type were delivered in the years 1982 to 1985. Her owner changed title again to Portnet Ltd, but by 2000 had been reorganised with the tugs passing to Transnet Ltd. At this point most of the fleet was renamed, and the **Otto Buhr** became **Umzumbe** by 2002, named after a town at the mouth of the Mzumbe River. The **Otto Buhr** was registered in East London, but is thought to have spent most of her working days at Durban, which is where we see her on 20 June 1996. As **Umzumbe** she was still owned by Transnet in 2013, but was put up for sale by auction that year.

(Nigel Jones)

Thailand, a country formerly-known as Siam, is located in south-east Asia on the Indochina peninsula. Its capital city is Bangkok and since 1985 has enjoyed a prosperous economy. The Port Authority of Thailand was founded in 1951 and was initially responsible for operations including towage at the river port at Bangkok, and from the 1960s, the new larger port at Laem Chabang. Other ports now controlled include Chieng Saen, Chiang Kong and Ranong. The **Tarua 108** is a harbour tug constructed in Germany in 1969 by D W Kremer Sohn GmbH & Co, Elmshorn, as the **Tarua 8** for the Port Authority of Thailand. She was of a similar design to the earlier **Tarua 5**, **Tarua 6** and **Tarua 7** which were built at a number of other German shipyards. She had a gross tonnage of 181 and was powered by a 1500bhp 6-cylinder MAN diesel. Her propulsion method is a single Voith Schneider cycloidal unit, although her lines do not follow those of a typical tractor tug. At some point prior to 2005 the **Tarua 7** and **Tarua 8** were renamed **Tarua 107** and **Tarua 108**. In this view dated 29 October 2005 the **Tarua 108** is underway at Bangkok. In 2012 the Port Authority of Thailand (Marine Department) took delivery of the modern ASD Z-drive tugs, the **Tarua 120** and **Tarua 302**, which were built locally.

(Simon Smith)

TOWAGE IN THE FAR EAST The Singapore anchorage provides the setting for this photograph of the **Goldpuller**, a former Dutch tug now in her last years of existence. She is without doubt a classic ocean-going tug of her era, and despite her age, appears to be in more or less original condition. The **Goldpuller** was launched 20 February 1951 by J & K Smit's Scheepswerven at Kinderdijk in the Netherlands as the **Oceaan** for the account of L Smit & Co's Sleepdienst NV, Rotterdam. She was similar to the **Rode Zee** of 1949 and was followed into service two years later by the **Oostzee**. She was 473 tons gross and had an overall length of 159 feet. Her main engine was a 6-cylinder MAN diesel of 2000bhp built by the shipyard, which gave her a speed of 12 knots. In 1968 she

came under the British flag and took up duties with her new owner Overseas Towage and Salvage Co Ltd, London, as **Salvonia**. Three years later she passed to Pacific Trade Navigation Co, Monrovia, and in 1973 to Straits Maritime Co Pte Ltd, of Singapore. Disaster struck for the first time in 1974 when she capsized and sank at Sattahip, Thailand, but was raised and returned to service with Limerick Investments Inc initially under the Liberian flag. In 1979 she became the **Goldpuller** for Red Sea & Gulf Pte Ltd, and sailing under the Singapore flag. She capsized and sank for a second time in June 1982 at Singapore. This time she was raised and broken up locally.

(Mike Lee [Andrew Wiltshire collection])

The Z-Peller azimuth propulsion system was developed over forty years ago by Niigata Engineering Co Ltd in Japan and started to feature in Japanese ship-handling tugs from the late 1960s. Its application to tugs on a worldwide scale was evident by the 1980s. The **Komaki Maru** of 1971 is a very good example of an early Z-Peller tug and at 199grt is a typical size for this period. She was built by Kanagawa Zosen at Kobe for Nagoya Kisen KK (Nagoya Kisen Kaisha Ltd.) of Nagoya and was their first Z-Peller propulsion tug, the first of many. Most early Japanese-built Z-Peller tugs featured Niigata diesel engines and the **Komaki Maru** had a 6-cylinder pair with an output of 2402bhp. This image shows her underway in the port at Nagoya on 28 January 1980. She was sold in 1999, passing initially to Tarassa, Osaka who renamed her **Tenyo Maru**. The following year she became the **Daiko Maru** for Tokyo Kinkai Yuso and finally the **Tenyo Maru No. 2** in 2001 for Techno Marine, Tokyo. By 2006 she had left Japan and was working in South Korea for Sea Green Co Ltd at Busan, and was still at work in 2012.

(Andrew Wiltshire)

North and South Vietnam were unified in 1975 under a Communist government and began a path towards economic recovery. The Saigon River in southern Vietnam flows for 140 miles into the Nha Be River and passes through Ho Chi Minh City which was formerly Saigon. The **Falcon 17** at first glance appears to be a fairly typical small tug of Asian origin, but this is not the case at all. She was built in France by Ch. Normands Réunis, Courseulles-sur-Mer, as the **Chien Thang 101**, for the Government of the Socialist Republic of Vietnam, one of a series of five identical shrimp trawlers. In 2006, along with the **Chien Thang 102**, she was rebuilt into a tug of 157grt, and both entered service with new owners Falcon Shipping Co (Cong Ty Co Phan Van Tai Dau Khi Viet Nam) as **Falcon 17** and **Falcon 18**, respectively. The hull of the **Falcon 17** was 87 feet in length with a breadth of 26 feet, and rather surprisingly the original machinery was retained. This consisted of a 12-cylinder Société Surgerienne de Construction Mécaniques-France (Poyaud) diesel of a mere 441bhp. The **Falcon 17** is seen moored on the Saigon River on 28 February 2012. This same owner also operates the tugs **Falcon 16** and **Falcon 21** and a fleet of bulk carriers.

(Simon Smith)

The **Natuna Tiger** was a purpose-built anchor-handling tug and is seen here at Mumbai on 29 December 1999. She was completed in 1980 as the **Gauntlet** for Australian owner International Offshore Services Pty, but by 1981 had passed to P&O International Offshore Services Pty, of Sydney, as **Lady Florence**. She was completed by the New South Wales Government Engineering & Shipbuilding Undertaking at Newcastle and has a gross tonnage of 760 and overall length of 144 feet. She is powered by two General Motors Electro-Motive diesels of 5752bhp driving a pair of controllable-pitch propellers. The **Natuna Tiger** has a speed of 12.5 knots and as can be seen by the symbol on her hull, she is fitted with a bow thruster unit. She became **Natuna Tiger** in 1993 when she was acquired by Natuna Richfield Maritime Pte Ltd of Singapore who also own the **Natuna Panther** of 1976, formerly the **Boa Power**. In 2013 the **Natuna Tiger** was still active with the same owner, and managed by Pacific Richfield Marine Pte Ltd.

(Nigel Jones)

The Republic of Indonesia is an archipelago in south-east Asia and made up of more than 17,000 separate islands. It is divided into six regions which include Java, Sumatra, Kalimantan and Sulawesi. Within Java we find the capital city and major port of Jakarta, and also the smaller port of Tanjung Emas at Semarang in central Java. In the 1980s, the Indonesian government placed in service eight modern tugs under the responsibility of the Ministry of Sea Communications at Jakarta. They were all built in Indonesia and took names numbered upwards from *Anggada VIII*. Two similar tugs were the *Anggada X* and *Anggada XI* which were delivered in 1986 from the yard of PT Kodja (Unit II), Jakarta, and had gross tonnages of 223 and 203, respectively. They were 95 feet in length with a beam of nearly 28 feet and were powered by a pair of 6-cylinder Niigata diesels of 1600bhp and driving twin fixed-pitch propellers. We see the *Anggada X* at Semarang in July 1988, where she was working with her sistership, the *Anggada XI*. The final five vessels in the series *Anggada XII* to *Anggada XVI* were delivered in 1988 and featured MWM engines. In 2013 the *Anggada X* was still in service by which time her owner was given as Indonesia Port Corp III, Surabaya.

(Brian Fisher)

Prior to 1973 the two principal tug operators at Hong Kong were Hong Kong and Whampoa Dock Co Ltd and the Taikoo Dockyard and Engineering Co of Hong Kong Ltd, both of which merged to form the Hong Kong Salvage and Towage Co Ltd. Since 1973 the fleet has benefitted from the regular addition of modern, powerful and versatile tugs, mainly for ship-handling at the port. A much larger tug was delivered in May 1986 from the Japanese yard of Imamura Zosen Shipbuilding Co Ltd, at Kure and took the name *Tai O*. At 411 tonnes gross, she was classed a multi-purpose stern-drive tug with fire-fighting capability, and her deployment in the South China Sea and Asia Pacific regions as a salvage tug was envisaged. Her main engines were two 6-cylinder Yanmar diesels of 4000bhp driving a pair of Duckpeller azimuthing propulsion units giving the *Tai O.* a bollard pull of approximately 53 tonnes. She had accommodation for twelve crew and was capable of cruising at 13.3 knots. The *Tai O.* is seen here in Hong Kong harbour during August 1988. In 1997 she transferred to the Panamanian flag and in 2000 was sold to Celtic Tugs Ltd, Cobh, who renamed her *Celtic Isle*. She was still in service in 2013 as such.

(Brian Fisher)

The motor tug *Gertak Sanggol* is seen operating at the port of Penang, a major seaport in Malaysia that has continued to develop for a number of decades, and which is responsible for the export of goods to more than 200 destinations worldwide. The *Gertak Sanggol* looks quite dated; the lines of her hull and superstructure almost resemble that of a steam tug. However, she was built in 1968 in Hong Kong by the Cheoy Lee Shipyard and has a gross tonnage of 199. She entered service as the *Tan Sri Sardon* for the Penang Port Commission, and changed her name to *Gertak Sanggol* in 1975. She is a twin-screw tug, and is powered by two 8-cylinder Lister Blackstone diesels of 1318bhp which give her a speed of 11 knots. In 1994 the Penang Port Commision was disbanded by the Malaysian government and placed in control of a privatised body with the title Penang Port Sdn Bhd. As the port developed, newer more powerful and versatile tugs were put into service. The *Gertak Sanggol* was sold by 2006 passing into another local fleet, Syarikat Lunar Shipping Sdn Bhd, and retaining the same name

(Andrew Wiltshire collection)

Flowing through the centre of Shanghai is the Huangpu River, which is itself a tributary of the Yangtze River and in turn flows into the East China Sea. Since the mid-1970s a large fleet of harbour tugs has been built up which includes many vessels that have names in the Hai Gang series. Most of these tugs are of Japanese origin, although exact details for some of them are hard to find. A relatively new vessel in this series is the **Hai Gang 27,** which is thought to date from the early 1990s. Of 337grt, she is generally of similar layout to the older vessel seen below with an overall length of 109 feet and a breadth of 32 feet. She is believed to have been acquired in the mid-1990s from her Japanese owners by the Shanghai Harbour Towing Corporation, for use in the Shanghai area. She is seen in dramatic lighting conditions at Shanghai on 24 November 2004. There are thought to have been at least seventeen tugs of similar design in the Hai Gang series, and dating from the 1970s to the 1990s including numbers 2, 10 and 24 to 26. More modern examples include the **Hai Gang 24** and **Hai Gang 53**. The **Hai Gang 27** remains active in 2013.

(Nigel Jones)

An earlier example is the **Hai Gang 12** that was completed in 1973. She is a Z-Peller type tug of 290grt and built by Ishikawajima Ship and Chemical Plant Co Ltd at Tokyo. She was originally the **Okitsu Maru** and operated for Mitomo Konpu Unyu KK of Yokohama. It is thought that she passed to the Chinese government in 1975 and was allocated to the Shanghai Port Affairs department as the **Hai Gang 12**. She is powered by a pair of 6-cylinder Daihatsu 6DSM26 diesels of 2600bhp and by 2009 was owned by Shanghai Harbour Fuxing Shipping, a subsidiary of Shanghai International Port Group (SIPG). She is seen on the Huangpu River, Shanghai, on 17 April 2009.

(Simon Smith)

BUILT IN THE UNITED KINGDOM The River Clyde has a strong affinity with the much-loved South African steam tugs with no fewer than seventeen examples being built at five different yards. Fergusons completed eight tugs between 1914 and 1961, with Lobnitz contributing six vessels in the 1930s. Single tug orders were placed with Inglis, W Simons and also Bow McLachlan and Co Ltd of Paisley who produced the fine-looking steam tug *T. S. McEwen* in 1925. She was launched on 23 April 1925 and delivered to the South African government (Railways and Harbours Administration) at Cape Town, and had a gross tonnage of 660. The *T. S. McEwen* was a coal-fired vessel powered by a pair of Bow McLachlan triple-expansion steam engines of 2800ihp. She was a twin-screw tug with a speed of 12 knots. By the 1930s her gross tonnage was increased to 792, and she soon earned herself the nickname *Smokey Sue* on account of her distinctive emissions. She was replaced in 1974 by the Voith Schneider tractor *J. H. Botha* and subsequently laid up at Cape Town with the intention of selling her for preservation. By June 1977 she had been moved to Durban and stripped. The *T. S. McEwen* was eventually returned to Cape Town under tow, and scuttled five nautical miles off Robben Island in Table Bay, on 9 June 1977. This view of her at Cape Town dates from 1969.

(Trevor Jones)

Brindisi is a city and port located on the Adriatic Sea in the south-east of Italy. The long established tug operator at Brindisi has been Fratelli Barretta which continues to serve the port in 2013 with six vessels. In 1969 the Alexandra Towing Co Ltd steam tugs *Canada* and *Formby* of 1951 were acquired by Fratelli Barretta, and became the *Strepitoso* and *Poderoso*, respectively. This was a period when many British-owned steam tugs that had become redundant, found further use in either Italian or Greek waters. The last steam tugs built for service in the United Kingdom were the *North* tugs of Alexandra Towing. When these came on the market in 1972/73 all seven passed to Italian owners. The *North Buoy* and *North Wall* dated from 1959 and served at Liverpool until 1969 when

they were transferred to Swansea. They were built on the Clyde by Scott and Sons (Bowling) Ltd and were 211grt oil-fired vessels of 1000ihp. In 1973 they were sold to Fratelli Barretta fu Domenico and renamed *Coraggioso* and *Maestoso*. The *Maestoso* is seen at Brindisi in October 1981 hard at work turning a ferry. By 1986 her owner was named as Impresa Fratelli Barretta – Domenico e Giovanni Barretta snc, but her days were now numbered. The 1980s was to be the final decade for most Italian steam tugs, and all four Barretta tugs mentioned above were out of use by 1988. The *Maestoso* passed to Comifer Srl, Brindisi, in December 1988 for scrap along with the *Coraggioso*.

(Pete Brabham)

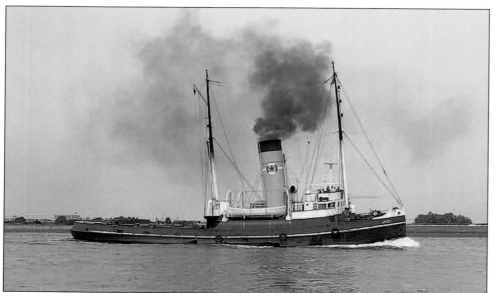

In July 1971, the Yugoslav-flag tug **Smjeli** is seen a long way from home as she makes her way along the New Waterway. However, she does make a fine sight as she belches out some black smoke from her oil-fired boiler. The **Smjeli** had an Amos and Smith triple-expansion steam engine of 1350ihp which gave her a service speed of 10 knots. She was an Empire-type tug of the Englishman/Larch class which was based on the steam tug **Englishman** of 1937, and intended for coastal service. Eight examples were constructed, split equally between the yards of Clelands (Successors) Ltd on Tyneside and Goole Shipbuilding and Repairing Co Ltd in Yorkshire. The **Smelji** was launched on 30 January 1941 as **Empire Larch**, one of the Goole-built tugs, which were all put under the management of United Towing Co Ltd of Hull. By the end of World War Two only the **Empire Larch** survived from the Goole quartet, and with involvement in the Normandy landings in 1944 to her credit, was sold to United Towing Co Ltd in April 1946 becoming the **Masterman**. In 1962 she was sold to Brodospas Poduzece za Spasavanje i Teglenje Brodova, Split, and placed under the Yugoslav registry as **Smjeli**. She was withdrawn from service by her owner in 1973, who then broke her up at Sveti Kajo in November that year.

(Andrew Wiltshire collection)

John Howard and Co Ltd was a civil and marine engineering contractor that was involved in a number of major projects around the UK in the 1960s and 1970s. This included projects at the ports of Liverpool and Felixstowe and also work on the Severn and Humber bridges. They operated a number of tugs including six motor tugs built new in the UK between 1968 and 1973. Five of these were completed by Richards Shipbuilders at Lowestoft and were between 148 and 151grt. The first pair completed in 1968 were the **Alison Howard** and the **Lady Howard**. They were followed by **Elizabeth Howard** in 1969, **Alison Howard II** in 1972 and **Susie Howard** in 1973. The final tug was the larger **Lady Howard II** from the yard of Fellows at Great Yarmouth, and all had been sold on for further service by 1975. The first three mentioned were sold to Gray Mackenzie & Co Ltd, London in 1971 for service in the Middle East. The **Lady Howard** became the **Al Qader** and later from 1982 the **Gray Beaver** for Gray Marine Services under the flag of Bahrain. At some later date she gained the name **Saad 7** before becoming the **Shaima** for Juma Abu Sheikha under the United Arab Emirates (UAE) flag registered at Sharjah. This is how we see her at Mumbai in India on 29 December 1997. She is still believed to be sailing under this name in 2013.

(Nigel Jones)

Igoumenitsa provides a tranquil setting on 20 September 2004 for the Greek motor tug **Thiella**, a British-built vessel dating from 1962, and registered at Kerkyra. The **Thiella** began life as the **Alnmouth** for France, Fenwick Tyne & Wear Co Ltd, Newcastle, and named after a coastal village in Northumberland. Upon delivery she was chartered to Tyne Tugs Ltd for fifteen years and based on the River Tyne. The **Alnmouth** was very similar to Lawson Batey's **Appelsider**, which was also built at the same yard of Richard Dunston at Hessle on Humberside. However, the **Alnmouth** featured a Ruston and Hornsby main engine which had an output of 1080bhp. She was transferred to Lawson Batey

Tugs Ltd in 1977 and sold to Greek owners Thiela Shipping Co in 1987 and renamed **Thiela**. She changed hands the same year and became **Thiella** for Megalohari Hellenic Tugboats, whose fleet at one time consisted largely of former British tugs including well-known names like **Graygarth** of 1970 and **Trafalgar** of 1966. In 2001 the **Thiella** passed to Igoumenitsa Naftiki Eteria who went on to rename her **Thyella** in 2005. She is believed to still be in service as such in 2013.

(Nigel Jones)

Scott and Sons of Bowling on the Clyde built a number of steam tugs between 1948 and 1957 for service in the Persian Gulf area. In 1954 the Iraq government (Director General of Navigation) took delivery of the steam tug **Hazim** followed in 1957 by the **Hashim**. Both were intended for service on the Shatt al Arab waterway and at the oil port of Fao. They were large tugs at 462 tons gross and had a triple expansion steam engine of 1500ihp by Plenty and Son Ltd. In 1966 they were renamed **Furat** and **Dijlah** respectively, and the **Dijlah** is seen here on 5 May 1980 in the tranquil setting of the Shatt al Arab waterway. At this time, as well as operating a fleet of motor tugs, their owner, now restyled the Goverrnment

of Iraq, Basarah had three other steam tugs. These were the **Heet** of 1949, the former Empire tug **Al Zab** of 1945 and the elderly former Admiralty tug **Shu'Alah** of 1919. However, the last two were out of use and derelict at Basrah. The Iran-Iraq war during the 1980s, and subsequent conflicts, took its toll on all shipping on the Shatt al Arab waterway, and by 1997 the **Dijlah** had been laid up in a badly fire-damaged state near Basrah. Following the invasion of Iraq it is thought all government assets were seized and possibly destroyed, and in 2011 no tugs were listed by Lloyd's Register as being operated.

(Andrew Wiltshire)

The Alexandra Towing Co Ltd established a tug operation in Gibraltar in the late 1970s, which passed to Howard Smith in 1993 and was eventually taken over by the newly-founded T P Towage Co Ltd in 1998. An early vessel transferred from the UK mainland to Gibraltar was the **Deben** which was previously based at Felixstowe and was originally the London tug **Sun XXII** of 1960. Her sistership was the **Sun XXI** of 1959, which like the **Deben** had been built by Philip and Son Ltd, of Dartmouth, and had a grt of 183. They were both delivered new to W H J Alexander Ltd (Sun Tugs) of London and based on the Thames. In service with Alexandra Towing Co Ltd, London, from 1975, the **Sun XXI** was transferred to Southampton in the late 1970s before joining the **Deben** at Gibraltar in 1981. The **Deben** was wrecked off the coast of Morocco in June 1986, but the **Sun XXI** continued to work at Gibraltar until her sale in 1993 to local owner Lionel Ferro, who renamed her **Nicky**. In 1999 she passed to Straits Barge and Tug Co Ltd at Gibraltar and was broken up at Cadiz in Spain in 2003. In this view the **Sun XXI** has been recorded on 14 September 1990, with the Rock of Gibraltar in the background.

(Andrew Wiltshire)

TUGS ON RIVERS AND WATERWAYS We shall now take a look at some tugs working inland on rivers, canals, lakes and inland waterways. The **Stevns Iceflower** is a Danish-owned tug that was completed in January 2006 by the East Isle Shipyard Ltd of Georgetown, Canada, and was followed into service by her sister, the **Stevns Icecap**. Both are modern azimuthing stern drive (ASD) tugs of 381grt and built to Ice Class 1A standard. The **Stevns Iceflower** features two remotely controlled water/foam monitors for fire-fighting, and a Kamewa bow thruster unit. Propulsion is by means of a pair of Aquamaster US255 units, and power for these is obtained from two 16-cylinder Caterpillar diesels of 5052bhp, which give her a bollard pull of 60.4 tonnes ahead and 56.9 tonnes astern. The

Stevns Iceflower was built for Stevns Multi Ships II (Nordane Shipping A/S) of Denmark and in 2007 was chartered to Svitzer as the **Svitzer Njord** reverting to her original name in 2008. The **Stevns Iceflower** is seen here on the Kiel Canal in the spring of 2007. In 2009 she passed to Rio Tinto Alcan Inc for operation at a terminal at Port Alfred in eastern Canada and took the new name **Fjord Saguenay**. Her sister, the **Stevns Icecap** followed suit in 2011 becoming the **Fjord Eternite**. In 2009 two new and similar tugs were built for Nordane Shipping, the **Stevns Icequeen** and a new **Stevns Iceflower**, and were followed in 2010 by the similar **Stevns Battler** and **Stevns Breake**r.

(Douglas Cromby)

E N Bisso & Son Inc, of New Orleans, has been providing towage services on the lower Mississippi for well over one hundred years. In more recent times they began to serve Gulfport, and now undertake coastal towing in the Gulf of Mexico. In 2013 a fleet of fourteen tugs is maintained. In October 1992 we see the **Susan W.** underway on the Mississippi. She joined the Bisso fleet in 1985 having previously been the **El Mulo Grande** of Twenty Grand Offshore Inc (Tidewater Inc). A tug of 167 tons gross she was built in 1966 by Universal Iron Works Inc at Houma. She was originally powered by a single 1800bhp diesel engine, but was later refitted with a pair of Caterpillar diesels of 2000bhp, which gave her a bollard pull of 24 tonnes. After just ten years service in the E N Bisso fleet the **Susan W.** was sold to the Dominican Republic for service with Remolcadores Dominicanos SA, Santo Domingo, as the **Hispaniola**. She was still sailing as such in 2012.

(René Beauchamp)

We now visit the North American Great Lakes where we find a well-known former British tug putting in good service for her owner. The **Avenger IV** arrived in Canada in 1985 after being sold by Alexandra Towing Co Ltd of London to Purvis Marine Ltd of Sault Ste Marie, Ontario, and this view of her dates from 16 May 1991. She was originally the **Avenger**, launched in 1962 by Cochrane & Sons Ltd, Selby, for The Elliott Steam Tug Co (1949) Ltd, London. She was one of a pair of identical tugs built to provide towage and fire-fighting cover at the oil tanker terminals at Coryton and Canvey Island, her sister being the **Hibernia** delivered to William Watkins Ltd in 1963. As such they featured a large tripod mast supporting fire-fighting monitors and were quite large tugs at around 293grt. The **Avenger** passed to William Watkins in 1965 and London Tugs Ltd in 1969. In 1974 she was fitted with a controllable-pitch propeller and a Kort nozzle which saw her bollard pull rise from 18 to 32 tonnes. The London Tugs fleet was taken over by Alexandra Towing Co Ltd in 1975 and gradually modernised. After her sale to Purvis Marine the **Avenger** was renamed **Avenger IV** and had a wheelhouse built onto what was her fire-fighting platform. In 2013 she was still in service with Purvis Marine.

(Andrew Wiltshire collection)

The **CSPLO Orlik** was an unusual inland stern-wheel motor paddle tug that was built in 1951. She was designed as a shallow draught vessel, but had to be narrow to pass through the locks on the River Vltava. Four prototypes appeared in the 1930s followed by eight similar tugs in the early 1950s. The **CSPLO Orlik** was delivered to CSPLO - Czechoslovak Elbe Oder Navigation National Company at Prague having been built at Melnik, near Prague. She displaced 50 tons and had an overall length of 188 feet, but a draught of a mere two feet. In 1957 she was re-engined, which gave her a new output of 550bhp, and this is how we see her near Dresden in June 1991. The **CSPLO Orlik** was sold to Dutch owner "Veka Scheepvaart & Handelsonderneming BV" at Werkendam in 2001, and registered at Rotterdam thereafter. Now believed to be named simply **Orlik**, she was known to still exist in 2007, and may now be in preservation. A number of the other 1950s-built sister tugs still survive, with at least three thought to be in the Prague area.

(Nigel Jones)

Seven new motor tugs were ordered by CSPLO - Czechoslovak Elbe Oder Navigation National Company in the late 1950s to replace much older steam tugs that were proving unreliable in service on the Elbe and Vltava rivers. The new vessels were used for towing barges between Stfiekov and Cologne on the River Elbe, and Melnik and Prague on the River Vltava; and were delivered between 1958 and 1961. They were named after musicians, but from 1964 received numbers **R-1** to **R-7**. These unusual tugs were 103 feet in length and had a welded hull built to work in ice conditions. They were twin-screw vessels for manoeuvrability and were powered by a pair of turbo-charged Skoda diesels with a total output of 390bhp. All seven vessels received modifications over the years including a pushing knee added to the stem, and the tugs were moved about to address changes in trade. When the **R-2** became redundant, she passed to an owner in Prague, but was later scrapped. Of the six other tugs in this class, five still exist in 2013, and four of them **R-3**, **R-4**, **R-5** and **R-7** are still at work with new owners. The subject of our photograph is the **CSPLO R-2** and she is seen at Prague in August 1970 with a coal barge in tow. When new she was given the name **Antonín Dvořák** after the Czech-born composer.

(John Wiltshire collection)

The Suez Canal was opened for navigation in November 1869 and a fleet of tugs has been maintained for over one hundred years. The Suez Canal Authority was formed in 1956 and currently operates a fleet of around thirty tugs which are used for towing and berthing of ships as well as fire-fighting, escort and salvage work. In 1976 the first of eight virtually new Z-peller tugs was purchased from Japanese owners and they took the names *Moawen 1* to *Moawen 8*. They were followed in 1978 by six large purpose-built Voith tractor tugs from the yard of Hayashikane Shipbuilding & Engineering Co Ltd, of Nagasaki. These solid-looking tugs had a gross tonnage of 362 and hull dimensions of 118 feet overall length with a breadth of 38 feet. One of these vessels, the *Baher /2* is seen underway on the Suez Canal on 21 September 1994. She features a pair of Voith Schneider 32G11/200 propulsion units driven by two 16-cyl MTU diesels of 3800bhp giving a bollard pull of 45 tonnes. The *Baher /2* alongwith her sisters *A. Bahgat*, *F. Bakr*, *Bareh /2*, *Basel /2* and *Batal /2* were still in service in 2013.

(Nigel Jones)

There are hundreds of pusher-tugs in use on the inland waterways in Europe and they vary in size greatly. Some are converted from conventional tugs but many are purpose-built vessels. Some of these are large long-range tugs like the **Albert Auberger** which has been designed to operate with a raft of large barges over great distances. She was built in 1982 by De Biesbosch at Dordrecht for French owner Compagnie Française de Navigation Rhénane SA and was registered in Strasbourg and intended for use on the Rhine. The **Albert Auberger** has a gross tonnage of 199 and a draught of just 6 feet 6 inches. She is 131 feet in length, with a breadth of 42 feet and is fitted with two large pusher-knees. In common with many other large pusher-tugs, she is a triple-screw vessel and is powered by three Deutz diesels which gave her a total power output of 6000bhp. In 2007 she was sold to German owner Imperial Reederei GmbH of Duisburg and renamed **Herkules II**. The **Albert Auberger** is seen while being slipped at Duisburg in March 2003.

(Dominic McCall)

Venezuela is located on the north coast of South America and has a number of ports along its coastline. It is also one of the world's largest oil producers with reserves located in the Orinoco Basin and Lake Maracaibo areas. In 2011 the government operated a fleet of approximately five tugs, while private fleets can be found at La Guaira, Puerto Cabello, Puerto Ordaz and Maracaibo. Maritima Ordaz CA is one such tug fleet that is based at Puerto Ordaz on the Orinoco River in the Bolivar State. At least five tugs are known to have been owned including the **Luisa C.** of 1975 and the **Carla C.** of 1980, and all were built in the United States. The **Laura C.** was purchased new in 1982 and is a tug of 302grt built in Houma by the Main Iron Works Inc. She is quite unusual in that she is of triple-screw layout which although common in large inland pusher-tugs, is rare in conventional sea-going vessels. The **Laura C.** is powered by three 16-cylinder General Motors Detroit Diesel engines with a total power output of 2790bhp that give her a speed of 12 knots. She is seen at Puerto Ordaz in December 1989 and is still in service in 2013.

(Brian Fisher)

The French city and port of Caen is to be found in Lower Normandy and is located approximately six miles inland. Caen is accessed via the Caen Canal which runs from the ferry port at Ouistreham. In 1969 the first of a pair of identical motor tugs the *Ingénieur Maxime Hesse* was completed at the Calais shipyard of SOCARENAM. She was delivered to Société de Gerance de Navigation (SOGENA) at Caen in January that year, and has a gross tonnage of 135. She is powered by a 6-cylinder Atlas-Mak diesel of 1400bhp which drives a fixed-pitch propeller in a Kort nozzle. The name *Ingénieur Maxime Hesse* was actually abbreviated to *Ing. Maxime Hesse* on the tug herself as can be seen in this view taken in July 1985 along the Caen Canal. Her sistership was delivered in 1971 as the *Appelant*, and both tugs had a similar bollard pull of 25 tonnes. The *Ingénieur Maxime Hesse* passed to AUXPORT Société Auxiliaire Portuaire, Brest, in 1994 and was renamed *Abeille Iroise*. She later came under the ownership of Les Abeilles SA at Brest, who in 2007 were taken over by Spanish tug operator Groupo Boluda. In 2008 she became the *VB Iroise* and was still sailing as such in 2012. Back at Caen, the *Appelant* passed to Chambre de Commerce et d'Industrie de Caen in 2001, and renamed *Caen Ouistreham 2*. In 2011 she was still hard at work, and was in service alongside the Voith tractor tug *Caen Ouistreham III*.

(Bernard McCall)

OCEAN-GOING TUGS The USSR is known to have had a class of twelve single-screw, ocean-going salvage tugs of 828 gross tons, and fitted with diesel-electric propulsion. They were built for civilian service between 1959 and 1962, although it is possible that there were further examples in naval service. The class included vessels such as the **Atlas**, **Poseydon**, **Hermes** and the subject of our image the **Atlant**. The **Atlant** is seen at Singapore on 17 February 1980, and her hull is starting to look rather uncared for, which was not untypical of many seagoing Russian tugs at this time. The **Atlant** was new in 1959 and her overall length was 171 feet and her beam was just less than 38 feet. Her hull was built to navigate in icy waters, and she was powered by two 6-cylinder Penza diesels.

These were coupled to a pair of generators which supplied power to a single electric motor, and in turn drove the single propeller giving her a speed of 13.5 knots. We cannot be exactly sure where she was built, but another member of the class, the **Kapitan V. Fedotov** was completed at Kaliningrad in the USSR by the Yantar Shipyard. It is therefore quite likely that the entire class came from this yard. As the year 1980 dawned, eleven of the class were still in existence, and by 1986 the **Atlant** was recorded as being owned by USSR – Black Sea Shipping Co, Odessa. It was under the Ukraine flag that she was last known to have sailed.

(Don Brown)

The Chinese made quite a late entry into ocean towing, but did so in style in 1979/80. It was then that they took delivery of six large ocean-going salvage tugs. The largest vessels were the *De Da* and *De Yue*, which were built in Japan by Ishikawajima Harima Heavy Industries and at 3356grt, 321 feet overall length and with a bollard pull of around 200 tonnes were impressive tugs to say the least. They were instantly recognisable by the large goalpost mast and derricks directly in front of the superstructure. Four smaller salvage tugs were the *De An*, *De Li*, *De Ping* and *De Shun* which were completed by Wang Tak Engineering & Shipbuilding Co Ltd, Hong Kong and had a grt of 1186. It is thought that originally six tugs were planned, but only these four actually emerged. They were twin-screw vessels powered by two 6-cylinder diesels by Niigata Eng Co Ltd, and developed 6000bhp. The output was via a pair of controllable-pitch propellers which gave these tugs a very useful bollard pull of 85 tonnes and a service speed of 14 knots. In this view we see the *De Ping* of 1979 at anchor in Singapore Roads on 26 June 1999. She was then wearing the colours of the Shanghai Salvage Co, Shanghai with whom she had been operating since about 1985. In 2012 the *De Li* still sails under this name while the other three have new names and roles under the Chinese flag. Since 2004, the *De Ping* has been a salvage and rescue ship named *Dong Hai Jiu 159* for the Chinese government (Donghai Rescue).

(Nigel Jones)

West German tug and salvage company Bugsier-, Reederei-und Bergungs- AG of Hamburg received four new salvage tugs in the years 1972 to 1975. These large and handsome vessels were the *Wotan* (1972), *Simson* (1973), *Titan* (1974) and *Atlantic* (1975). All were built at the Bremerhaven yard of Schichau-Unterweser AG and were approximately 1599grt with an overall length of 253 feet and a breadth of 44 feet. They were twin-screw tugs powered by a pair of 12-cylinder vee-type Deutz diesels, which developed 8800bhp and drove a pair of controllable-pitch propellers giving a bollard pull of around 105 tonnes. In 1979 the *Titan* was fitted with fixed Kort nozzles, while her engines were uprated to a new total output of 13920bhp, giving a revised bollard pull of 135 tonnes. The *Wotan* was lost in 1990 after being struck by her tow, and subsequently the remaining three tugs were sold off. The *Titan* was sold in December 1992 to Vietnamese interests. This turned out to be the Vietnamese Navy and her official owners are described as Vietnammarine (Van Xuan Company) of Hanoi. She retained her original name *Titan*, and is seen here nearly twenty years later on 28 February 2012, at anchor on the Dong Nai River which is off the Saigon River. She was operating out of a small naval facility to the east of Cat Lai Container Terminal.

(Simon Smith)

The **Salviscount** was an attractive-looking British-built ocean-going tug that came from the yard of Robb Caledon Shipbuilders Ltd, of Leith. She was ordered by United Towing Co Ltd, of Hull, and boasted a number of innovative features in her compact design. She was launched on 19 September 1971 as the **Lloydsman**, and had a gross tonnage of 2041 and overall length of 264 feet. She normally had a crew of twenty-five, and was fitted for fire-fighting and carried a wide range of salvage equipment. Her propulsion consisted of a Kamewa controllable-pitch propeller incorporated in a Towmaster propulsion and steering system. She had two 10-cylinder vee-type Crossley-Pielstick main engines of 16000bhp at 500rpm, which gave her a speed of 18 knots and a maximum bollard pull of 150 tonnes. As well as towage worldwide with United Towing, she was also involved in the Icelandic Cod Wars in the 1970s. After less than a decade with her original owner, the **Lloydsman** was sold in 1980 to Selco Singapore Pte Ltd. and took the name **Salviscount**, joining many other large salvage tugs in this smart fleet. She is at anchor at Hong Kong in this view dated November 1983. As the **Salviscount** her working life was relatively brief and, in 1988 she arrived at Gadani Beach for scrapping, after a working career of just seventeen years.

(David Salisbury)

Two tugs delivered to the South African Marine Corporation during 1976 were the largest and most powerful tugs in the world at that time. The first to be handed over was the **S. A. Wolraad Woltemade** in April 1976, and was named after a local hero who died rescuing sailors from a wreck in Table Bay in June 1773. At 2822grt she was constructed at the Leith yard of Robb Caledon Shipbuilders Ltd, and her hull measured a massive 310ft overall length with a breadth of 50ft. Her sistership, completed in November, was built in Durban and christened **S. A. John Ross**. The **S. A. Wolraad Woltemade** was a single-screw salvge tug powered by a pair of 16-cylinder Mirrlees Blackstone diesels producing 19200bhp. These were geared to a controllable-pitch propeller operating in a fixed Kort nozzle and capable of achieving a maximum bollard pull of 210 tonnes and a speed of 20 knots. Both these tugs were placed on salvage station along the treacherous South African coast; should one of the many large tankers to navigate around the Cape of Good Hope get into difficulties. Both tugs lost the *S. A.* prefix to their names when placed under the Bermudan flag by 1979, and in 1983 both were sailing under the Panamanian flag. In 2010 the **Wolraad Woltemade** was renamed **Icon**, her working days over, and she was despatched to Indian shipbreakers at Alang. Here we see her arriving at Durban on 20 June 1996.

(Nigel Jones)

The **Hyundai T. No. 1002** is a large salvage tug that has sailed under the South Korean flag for most of her working life, albeit under many different names. She was launched in 1976 in Japan by Miyoshi Zosen KK, Uwajima, as the **Hoko Maru No. 7** along with her sister the **Hoko Maru No. 6**. They were completed the following year for Hyundai Shipbuilding Industries, of Ulsan, with the **Hoko Maru No. 7** becoming **Hyundai No. 110**. Both tugs were moved between owners in the Hyundai group, and by 1980 the **Hyundai No. 110** had been renamed **Chung Ryong No. 2** under the management of Asia Merchant Marine Co Ltd. In 1984 she became the **Hyundai T. No. 1002** with her owner stated as Hyundai Merchant Marine Co Ltd, Ulsan, while her sister became **Hyundai T. No. 1001**. As built, both tugs were powered by a pair of 8-cylinder Niigata 8MG40X diesels, but at some stage the **Hyundai T. No. 1002** was re-engined with two 6-cylinder Hanshin diesels of 9000bhp giving her a bollard pull of 120 tonnes. In this view **Hyundai T. No. 1002** is seen from the Lions Gate Bridge at Vancouver on 14 October 1989. Both tugs remained together when in 1998 they passed to the International Transport Contractors group for continued service. **Hyundai T. No. 1002** became **Sandy Cape**, while **Hyundai T. No. 1001** became **Sable Cape**. In 2007 **Sandy Cape** became **Sandy Pearl** for Yoshida Trading, Busan, and was still at work around the world in 2013.

(Rick Garcia)

This view of the **Fairplay XIV** was taken in the Bristol Channel on 17 June 1989. She was launched in November 1970 by F Schichau at Bremerhaven as the **Seetrans I** for Reederei ms "Seetrans I" FCH Stark KG at Hamburg and had a gross tonnage of 840. She was powered by two 8-cylinder Atlas-MAK diesels of 4786bhp driving a single fixed-pitch propeller in a Kort nozzle. The **Seetrans I** had a bollard pull of 56 tonnes and featured a bow thruster. Also completed at this time by F Schichau was a virtually identical vessel for Fairplay of Hamburg, the **Fairplay IX**. In 1975 the **Seetrans I** was sold to Raga Schiffahrtsgesellschaft mbH, Hamburg and put to work as the **Raga I**. By 1979 she had passed to Petersen and Alpers of Hamburg as **Hanseatic** and remained active until 1985 when she was laid up. Two years later she was purchased by "Fairplay Schleppdampfschiffsreederei Richard Bochard", Hamburg and given the new name **Fairplay XIV** which is how we see her here. Fairplay now had both of these similar tugs in their fleet, and during the 1990s reflagged both vessels to Antigua and Barbuda registry as a cost-cutting exercise. They now carried a Filipino crew, but still operated under German management. The **Fairplay XIV** was sold in 2007 to Diavlos Maritime, Piraeus, and became the **Pantodynamos** under the Panamanian flag. She was still in service in 2013.

(the late Mike Hawkins)

Smit International received four new ocean-going salvage tugs in 1975-77 which replaced older outdated tonnage. The **Smit Rotterdam** and **Smit London** were completed in 1975, and were followed by the slightly smaller pair **Smit New York** and **Smit Houston** in 1977. The **Smit London** was constructed at the yard of NV Scheepswerf & Machinefabriek "De Merwerde" v/h van Vliet & Co, Hardinxveld and delivered to Smit Internationale Zeesleep-en Bergingsbedrijf at Rotterdam. She had a gross tonnage of 2273 and an overall length of 245 feet. She relied on a pair of 9-cylinder Stork Werkspoor main engines of 13500bhp to drive her two controllable-pitch propellers which rotated in Kort nozzles. The **Smit London** transferred to the Bahamas flag in 1986, and was managed by Smit Tak International Ocean Towage and Salvage Co, of Nassau. In this view we see her at Halifax, Nova Scotia, on 21 December 1988. In 1991 her owner became SmitWijs Towage CV, Rotterdam and in 1998 she was renamed **SmitWijs London**. By 2005 she was sailing under the Singapore flag and in 2006 she passed to Wijsmuller Scheepsholding BV. In 2007 she was renamed **London** for Svitzer Ocean Towage, Rotterdam, and was stationed at Pasir Panjang, Singapore. 2013 was to be the final year for this well-travelled and much-admired tug. She was initially sold to Iliana Shipping Ltd as the **Global Change**, but shortly after arrived at Alang, India for breaking up on 1 June 2013.

(Mac Mackay - Tugfax)

International Transport Contractors (ITC) was formed in 1973 to manage the tugs and barges owned by Tschudi and Eitzen of Norway. They became involved in worldwide towage and salvage and eventually had offices in Tokyo and Houston, in addition to their head office at Haarlem in the Netherlands. In 1976 the first of seven large and well-equipped salvage tugs, the **Sirocco**, was delivered from her builder in Japan, followed soon after by the **Shamal**. Further examples were the **Santania**, **Simoon**, **Suhaili** and **Sumatras** in 1977, with the **Solano** completing the order in 1978. All seven tugs were registered in Panama from new. They were painted in an overall orange livery which made them very distinctive at this time, and could soon be found at work all around the world. This is a superb study of the **Sumatras** at Singapore on 12 June 2001. She had a gross tonnage of 846 and her hull an overall length of 180 feet with a breadth of 37 feet. The **Sumatras** was completed by Matsuura Tekko Zosen at Higashino, near Hiroshima, as a twin-screw fire-fighting salvage tug with a bollard pull of 110 tonnes. She was powered by two 16-cylinder vee-type Fuji diesels of 8200bhp which gave her a speed of 15.5 knots. In 1986 her registered owner was amended to International Transport Sotavento Inc and she retained the Panamanian registry. The **Sumatras** was sold to Industrial Transport Ltd, San Fernando, in 2011 and renamed **Rosalind Mary I**.

(Douglas Cromby)

The **Anglian Princess** was the first of two sisterships to be built in China for Klyne Tugs (Lowestoft) Ltd, and intended for service with the Maritime and Coastguard Agency (MCA). In 2001 Klyne Tugs was awarded the contract to provide four Emergency Towing Vessels (ETVs) to be stationed around the coast of Great Britain with the aim of preventing major marine accidents and the resulting pollution. The **Anglian Princess** was completed in July 2002 by the Yantai Raffles Shipyard Co Ltd of Yantai and entered service in the September. She is an anchor-handling supply tug of 2258grt with a bollard pull of 180 tonnes and capable of fire-fighting. Her two main Wärtsilä 16V32D engines produce a total of 16316bhp which drive controllable-pitch propellers that rotate in fixed nozzles. The **Anglian Princess** was stationed at Falmouth, while her sister the **Anglian Sovereign** which was delivered to Klyne in August 2003, was on station off the north-east coast of Scotland. In 2008 Klyne Tugs were taken over by J P Knight (Lowestoft) Ltd, and in September 2011 the provision of ETVs by the MCA was ended due to government budget cuts. In 2012 the **Anglian Princess** and **Anglian Sovereign** were sold to Smit Shipping Singapore Pte Ltd and managed by Smit Transport Belgium NV. They were duly renamed **Union Princess** and **Union Sovereign**. In her Klyne Tugs days, the **Anglian Princess** is seen anchored off Plymouth on 15 October 2005.

(Dominic McCall)

TOWAGE IN CARIBBEAN AND SOUTH AMERICAN WATERS The Barbados Port Authority is the provider of towage at the port of Bridgetown in Barbados. In 2013 two modern tugs, the *Pelican II*, a Damen Stantug 3909 of 1994, and the *Barbados II*, a Damen ASD 3110 of 2002, are used to assist shipping within the confines of the port. Both are fitted for fire-fighting, salvage and rescue work. They replaced the older British-built *Pelican* of 1961, and the *Barbados* of 1972 which was completed in the United States. The *Barbados II* has a gross tonnage of 313 and a length of 101 feet. Her hull was built in Russia by PO Sevmash Predpriyatiye at Severodvinsk and was towed to the Netherlands to be completed by BV Scheepswerf Damen at Gorinchem. The completed vessel was powered by two 6-cylinder Caterpillar 3606TA diesels developing 5520bhp and driving a pair of azimuthing thrusters giving the tug a bollard pull of 75 tonnes and a speed of 12.5 knots. This photograph of the *Barbados II* was taken at Bridgetown on 5 February 2012.

(Andrew Wiltshire collection)

The port of Puerto Montt is to be found in southern Chile and experienced much prosperity due to the rapid expansion of the salmon fishing industry in the 1990s. Its produce is exported to destinations all around the world. Towage at the port is provided by CPT Empresas Maritimas SA which also serves other ports in Chile, including Talcahuano and Tocopilla. They operate up to sixteen tugs which includes the former German vessels **Widder** of 1962 and **Helgoland** of 1970. The parent company is CPT Remolcadores SA with its origins going back to 1909, and which also provides towage at installations in Peru with its subsidiary Inmarsa, and Ecuador with subsidiary Sagemar. The **Tumbes** is a twin-screw tug completed in 2000 by President Marine Pte Ltd at Singapore and is similar to the **Lauca** and **Tepual** of 1997, which also operate for CPT in Chile. The **Tumbes** has a gross tonnage of 247 and an overall length of 95 feet. She is powered by a pair of 12-cylinder Caterpillar diesels which develop a total of 3152bhp and has a bollard pull of around 40 tonnes. Her owner is recorded as Santiago Leasing SA, Valparaiso, with CPT Empresas Maritimas SA as her managers. The **Tumbes** is photographed at Puerto Montt on 10 February 2013.

(Jim McFaul)

The Republic of Colombia is a country in north-west South America and has ports on both its Caribbean and North Pacific Coasts. Cartagena de Indias is the fifth largest city and is also a port located on the Caribbean; and is served by tugs of the Remolques y Transportes Maritimos Ltda (RETRAMAR) fleet. RETRAMAR is now part of the Coremar Group and has been serving the ports of Colombia since 1958. A number of tugs are stationed at Cartagena, and in 1999 these included the much-rebuilt twin-screw tug **Medoro** which dates from 1942. She was built on the Mississippi in the United States as the **ST48 Reeves** by the Dubuque Boat and Boiler Works, Dubuque, Iowa. She was transferred to the US Army Corps of Engineers in 1946 and renamed **Fort Norfolk**, before passing into civilian service in 1953 as **Patricia J.** for Able Marine Services, of New York. In 1954 she passed to St George Towing becoming **Walter Tracy** and continued to work for them until 1970. She was eventually sold to Colombian owners in 1981 as **Rio Manzanares**, becoming **Medoro** for RETRAMAR in 1992. It is not known when she was rebuilt, but at some stage she lost her original Atlas-Imperial diesels for a pair of 12-cylinder Caterpillars which then boosted her bhp to 2150. She was still putting in good service with RETRAMAR in 2011, having been transferred to Santa Marta in 2008. Here the **Medoro** is seen at Cartagena de Indias on 11 October 1999.

(Harry Cutter)

Cuba, a large island located in the Caribbean Sea, has a number of ports the main one being Havana, the capital city. In 1996 the first of two new tugs was completed for service at the port and operated under the Cypriot flag. The **Caribbean Storm** entered service with owner Dobletto Shipping Co Ltd, and was managed by Empresa de Navegacion Caribe and registered in Limassol, to be followed by the **Sea Wolf** in 1997. They have a gross tonnage of 131 and are 73 feet in length with a beam of just less than 24 feet. Both vessels were completed in Cuba by the yard of Damex Shipbuilding & Engineering AVV at Santiago de Cuba which has since built a number of other tugs for service in other ports around the world. The **Caribbean Storm** and **Sea Wolf** are twin-screw tugs each powered by a pair of 6-cylinder Caterpillar diesels of 1920bhp. The **Caribbean Storm** is seen at Havana on 24 March 1997, and both vessels were still with the same owner in 2013.

(Nigel Jones)

The Bahamas is located in the Atlantic Ocean to the north of Cuba and is made up of more than 700 islands. It was a British colony from 1718 until 1973 and the main port is Nassau. In 1980 the port authority under the Government of the Commonwealth of the Bahamas placed in service at Nassau two new twin-screw tugs that had been completed in the Netherlands. They were named **Grouper** and **Turbot** after breeds of fish and were 162grt. The **Grouper** was built by Bodewes Schpsw Volharding at Foxhol while the **Turbot** was from the yard of Rilaco BV at Krimpen. They were both 86 feet in length and had a pair of Caterpillar Tractor diesels of 2800bhp, and were capable of fire-fighting. They were joined in 1988 by the virtually identical tug **Snapper** and in 1990 by the much larger **Amberjack** which was 4690bhp, both coming from Dutch yards of Scheeps Damen BV. In the last twenty-five years Nassau has become a major cruise ship destination, but many of these vessels can navigate without the services of the Port Authority tugs. By 2011 it was known that the **Grouper** had been sold, and that only the **Snapper** and **Amber Jack** remained in service at Nassau. The **Turbot** was last reported in 2010 but was still very active at Nassau when this photograph was taken on 16 October 1999.

(Harry Cutter)

After being controlled by the Spanish, Jamaica in the Caribbean was under British rule from 1655 until gaining its independence in 1962. The main port at Kingston was operated by the Jamaican government department, the Kingston Harbour Authority and, in more recent years, containerisation has seen much expansion to cater for larger ships, and also for the cruise ship market. Two new tugs were acquired in 1979/80, and were constructed at the Norwegian shipyard of P Hoivolds M/V A/S of Kristiansand. The **Montego Bay** arrived in 1979 followed in 1980 by the **Port Antonio**. They were single-screw vessels of 186grt and overall length of 97 feet. They were each powered by a 16-cylinder General Motors Electro-Motive Division diesel of 2799bhp giving them a bollard pull of 37 tonnes, and were each fitted with a bow thruster unit. The **Montego Bay** is seen at Kingston on 15 May 1989. She was sold in 1998 to Venecia Ship Services CA (VESCA) of Puerto Cabello, Venezuela and became **Vesca R-20**, while the **Port Antonio** followed her the same year becoming **Vesca R-21**. Towage at Kingston is now undertaken by Maritime Towing Company Ltd using the powerful 305grt tugs **Port Maria** of 1996 and **Ocho Rios** of 1997.

(Jeff Screeton)

For decades there have been a large number of tugs operating in Brazil and two companies that come to mind are Saveiros, Camuyramo Servicos Maritimos SA and Wilson, Sons Servicos Maritimos SA. Another operator Empresa de Portos do Brasil SA (PORTOBRAS) had over twenty tugs at one time and many of these were completed in the 1970s. A good example of one of these tugs is the **Corumba** of 251grt and completed in 1978. She was built at Manaus on the Amazon river by "Estanave" Estaleiros Amazonia and was one of several similar vessels. She is seen at Maceio on 23 August 1986, a port and city in the Alagoas state south of Recife. The **Corumba** is a single-screw tug with two MAN-type Mecanica Pesada diesel engines with a total output of 2472bhp and has an overall length of 92 feet. Since 2007 her gross tonnage has changed to 181 for some reason, and her owner in more recent times is recorded as Sulnorte Servicios Maritimos Ltda of Rio de Janeiro, but she is still registered in Maceio. In 2013 there are many significant newer tug operators in Brazil, using more modern vessels.

(Andrew Wiltshire collection)

Maruba has been in the shipping business in Argentina for over fifty years, and currently operates around ten tugs at ports including Buenos Aires, Campana, Quequén-Necochea and Villa Constitucion. There are now quite a few Japanese-built Z-Peller stern drive tugs operating in Argentina and the **Observador** operating at Buenos Aires for Maruba SCA Empresa de Navegacion Maritima is a good example. She was completed in 1998 by Kanagawa Zosen KK at Kobe as the **Iwaki Maru** for Fukushima Kaiun KK Ltd. With a gross tonnage of 253, she has an overall length of 109 feet, a speed of 14 knots and accommodation for seven persons. Her machinery comprises a pair of 6-cylinder Niigata 6L28HX-type diesels of 3600bhp, driving two Z-Peller propulsion units. In 2002 she was renamed **Iide Maru** and in 2006 was sold to Serena Tanker Transport Inc under the Liberian flag and managed by Maruba SCA as the **Iide**. She became the **Observador** in 2007 for Maruba, which also operates the similar **Mirador** of 2000. She was the second tug to bear this name and is seen at Buenos Aires on 24 February 2013.

(Jim McFaul)

During the 1920s and early 1930s, a number of steam tugs were built at British, German and Italian shipyards for customers in Argentina. Some of these vessels had long working lives in Argentina, and many lasted in regular service until the late 1970s, at which point the Argentine government banned their use at Buenos Aires. Some were sold for further work while others were laid up, eventually being scrapped from 1992 onwards. At Puerto Galván three steam tugs owned by Satecna Costa Afuera SA could be found lying high and dry on the quayside. It had been the intention of the owner to preserve at least one of them, but the venture failed on grounds of cost. They were placed on the quay to prevent further legal problems as one had already sunk alongside. At Puerto Galván on 21 February 1994, we can make out four tugs. In the foreground on the left is the **Marsden** completed in 1923 by J P Rennoldson and Sons of South Shields for France, Fenwick Tyne and Wear Co Ltd of Newcastle. She was sold to Argentina in 1926. On the right is the **Restaurador** completed in 1929 by Smith's Dock Co Ltd of South Bank, and the funnel just visible behind belongs to the **Regidor** of 1928, both completed for The Argentine Navigation Co Ltd (N Mihanovich) Ltd of Buenos Aires. The grey tug also visible is the former Argentine Naval tug **Quilmes**. It is thought that all four tugs were scrapped in situ, around 2003/2004.

(Guillermo Berger)

We shall end our look at *"Tugs in Colour - Worldwide"* with a remarkable story of two survivors in Argentina. The steam tugs **Triunfador** and **Bio-Bio** had been working at the port of Quequén-Necochea, and ended their working days at the port of Santa Fe, approximately 475km upstream from Buenos Aires on the Paraná River. The **Triunfador** was completed in 1933 by A Hall & Co Ltd of Aberdeen as the **Nutria** for the Buenos Ayres Great Southern Railway Co. As such she had a gross tonnage of 213 and was very similar in many respects to the London tugs **Contest** and **Challenge** which came from the same yard in 1931 and 1933 respectively. The **Nutria** was completed as an oil-burning steam tug fitted with a triple expansion engine of 850ihp manufactured by the shipyard. She was sold in 1937 to Cia Argentina de Navegación Mihanovich Ltda and renamed **Triunfador**. In 1942 she transferred to Cía Argentina de Navegación Dodero and by 1959 was part of the state-owned fleet Flota Argentina de Navegación Fluvial.

The **Bio-Bio** was launched on 19 January 1942 by Cochrane & Sons Ltd, Selby, as the 277grt Hoedic class Empire tug **Empire Goblin**, and immediately delivered to South Africa for use as a rescue tug, and operated by the Union Government of South Africa. In 1948 she was purchased by Angel Gardella & Cía, an Argentinian company who were moving from fishing into ship towage. She was renamed **Bio-Bio** and by the mid-1950s was operating for Flota Argentina de Navegación Fluvial. Like the **Triunfador** she was oil-fired and her triple expansion engine of 825bhp was built by Amos & Smith Ltd, of Hull. Both the **Triunfador** and **Bio-Bio** were initially laid up in the early 1980s, and were part of a batch of redundant tugs purchased by Maruba SCA which put this pair back to work for a few more years. At Santa Fe they were laid up and kept under secure conditions which have ensured that they stayed intact to the present day. In 2011, the Histarmar Foundation (www.histarmar.org) was set up with one of its aims being to secure a future for these two steam tugs, by encouraging sponsorship etc. In 2012, Maruba SCA agreed to donate the two vessels for preservation providing that they were never used commercially again. However, and after considering all available options, the Histarmar Foundation is now pursuing its original project for **Triunfador** only. The plan is to move the vessel down river to Buenos Aires, where it could be displayed more prominently, and hopefully attract a sponsor for its eventual restoration. Both views were taken at Santa Fe on 25 October 2013.

(both photographs by Guillermo Berger)